THE WORLD'S EPOCH-MAKERS

EDITED BY

OLIPHANT SMEATON

# Anselm and

# His Work

By Rev. A. C. Welch, M.A., B.D.

PREVIOUS VOLUMES IN THIS SERIES :—

CRANMER AND THE ENGLISH REFORMATION.
By A. D. INNES, M.A.

WESLEY AND METHODISM.
By F. J. SNELL, M.A.

LUTHER AND THE GERMAN REFORMATION.
By Prof. T. M. LINDSAY, D.D.

BUDDHA AND BUDDHISM.
By ARTHUR LILLIE, M.A.

WILLIAM HERSCHEL AND HIS WORK.
By JAMES SIME, M.A., F.R.S.E.

FRANCIS AND DOMINIC.
By Prof. J. HERKLESS, D.D.

SAVONAROLA.
By Rev. G. M'HARDY, D.D.

*FOR COMPLETE LIST SEE END.*

# Anselm and

# His Work

By

## Rev. A. C. Welch, M.A., B.D.

New York.    Charles Scribner's Sons

1901

To

The Memory of

# A. C. W.

E'en as he trod that day to God so walked he from his birth
In simpleness and gentleness and honour and clean mirth

# PREFACE

A VOLUME of the size of the present does not permit
the insertion of references to authorities within the
text. It may be useful to indicate here the sources
from which I have drawn the view of Anselm's Life
and Times which is now presented. The classic
biography on which all later ones are based is that
by Eadmer. A monk of Canterbury, he became
Anselm's private secretary and confessor. He has
left to the world a study of his superior's private
life in the *De Vita et Conversatione Anselmi*, and of
his public conduct as archbishop in the *Historia
Novorum in Anglia*. I have been obliged to study
these in Gerberon's edition (Paris, 1675), and in
Migne's *Patrologia*: the best edition is that contri-
buted by Mr. Rule to the Rolls Series. Anselm was
also a voluminous correspondent, and over 400 of
his letters, private and official, have been preserved.
These I have consulted in Migne's *Patrologia* (clviii.–
ix.). It is unnecessary to catalogue the early chroniclers, Henry of Huntingdon, Orderic, and the rest.
They are the same for this period as for any other
in early English history. I would only single out
a contemporary Life of Gondulf of Rochester by an

unknown hand (Migne clix.), and the "Lives of the Abbots of Le Bec," by G. and M. Crispin in *Patres Ecclesiæ Anglicanæ*, Oxford 1845.

For the historical background and the general position of affairs in Europe I have found of special value the relative sections in Milman's *Latin Christianity*, Gregorovius' *Geschichte der Stadt Rom im Mittelalter*, Giesebrecht's *Geschichte der Deutschen Kaiserzeit*, and Montalembert's *Monks of the West*. The Life of Gregory VII. is still however a desideratum. There are many valuable facts relative to Normandy and especially to the condition of education there in *L'Abbaye du Bec et ses Écoles*, by Abbé Porée (Evreux, 1892). On the history of England nothing more is necessary than what our own historian has given; and Freeman in his *Norman Conquest* and the *Reign of William Rufus* has paid special attention to the ecclesiastical situation and to the work of Anselm. Palgrave's unfinished *Normandy and England* contains many brilliant suggestions. And some facts of value can be gleaned from H. Böhmer's *Kirche und Staat in England und in der Normandie im* XI. *und* XII. *Jahrhundert* (Leipzig, 1899).

Of monographs on Anselm there is no lack; and these are written from several points of view. The early volumes, Veder, *Dissertatio de Anselmo Cantuariensi* (Lugduni Batavorum, 1832), Möhler, *Anselm* (I have only seen a remarkably poor translation, London, 1842), and Franck, *Anselm von Canterbury* (Tübingen, 1842), are slight and inadequate sketches. Charma's *St. Anselme* (Paris, 1853) consists for the most part of extracts and of a bibliography which though out of date is still valuable. Hook treats of Anselm in his *Lives of the Archbishops of Canterbury*, but the High Church Anglican is too much irritated to be quite fair. Rémusat has a very brilliant life, *St. Anselme d'Aoste* (Paris, 1859), to which I acknowledge special indebtedness. Dean Church's *St. Anselm* almost ignores the theologian and thinker, but devotes special attention to the man and the ecclesiastic. Hasse's *Anselm von Canterbury* (Leipzig, 1852) contains in its volume on *Die Lehre* an elaborate and patient analysis of the doctrine. Martin Rule has published a voluminous *Life and Times of St. Anselm* (London, 1883). Rigg's *St. Anselm of Canterbury* (London, 1896) is marked by the virility of thought and individuality of judgment which characterise all his work. Finally a history of St. Anselm has been written by Père Ragey (Paris, N.D.). To this last I acknowledge a special debt. The author's acquaintance with the details of the ecclesiastical history makes his book a valuable commentary on the letters.

It is unnecessary to mention the treatises on philosophy and theology which deal with the Anselmic doctrine. It exercised so deep an influence that no later student has been able to ignore it.

I have to thank here Mr. G. W. Alexander, M.A., who has read the proofs, for this new evidence of an old kindness.

ADAM C. WELCH.

HELENSBURGH.

# CONTENTS

## CHAPTER IV

### THE MONOLOGIUM AND PROSLOGIUM

## CHAPTER V

### THE CHURCH IN ENGLAND: 1062–1087

## CHAPTER VI

### ELECTION AS ARCHBISHOP: 1092–1093

## CHAPTER VII

### ROCKINGHAM: 1093–1095

## CHAPTER VIII

### The Rupture at Winchester: 1095-1097

## CHAPTER IX

### The First Exile and "Cur Deus Homo": 1097-1098

## CHAPTER X

### Councils of Bari and Rome: 1098-1100

## CHAPTER XI

### The Investiture Question—Anselm and Beauclerk: 1100-1103

## CHAPTER XII

### THE CONCORDAT: 1103–1107

## CHAPTER XIII

### CONCLUSION: 1107–1109

# ANSELM AND HIS WORK

——◆——

## INTRODUCTION

EUROPE in the early half of that eleventh century into which Anselm was born was renewing itself under the influence of a quickened religious spirit. Christianity in the Western world had two great outward struggles with paganism, the first with a paganism which was already in possession and was rich in the accumulated treasures of an older civilisation, the second with a paganism which sought to repossess itself of Europe and to overwhelm in barbarism the new order almost before it had struck root. The early incursions which broke down the Roman Empire had hardly been survived, and their influence had not been assimilated, before an equally heavy storm burst upon the West. The Avars from Asia, ever fertile of men, thrust themselves into the centre of Europe, and wasting everything on their way penetrated through Austria. The Saracens already possessed North Africa, and had with difficulty been restricted within the limits of Spain; they had captured Sicily and were not unknown before the walls of Rome. The Danes had seized on

England: the last of England's missionaries to the Continent were fugitives from wrecked monasteries. From heathen Scandinavia the Normans had carved a cantle out of France, and were in no way content with the rich lands which they had won.

During several generations Christendom had seen one province after another of her territory torn away by aliens to her civilisation, her law, and her faith. The circle within which the light of a better order shone was small. And the light itself within the circle inevitably burned more dimly. Men needed all their strength for war. They were compelled to fight for standing-ground on behalf of the truths and institutions which they had already made their own. They had neither time nor energy left to rethink those truths or to reshape those institutions. To protect themselves against the enemy from without was their prime concern, and all their effort in thought as well as in deed was turned in that direction. Society had come to be constituted on a basis of war. Its recognition was given to those who could fight, its rewards to those who had fought well. Even the institutions which owed their inception to a different purpose were influenced by the same spirit. The Church was secularised. The bishops often became ministers of State, partly because there were no others who had the capacity to fulfil that necessary function, still more because it was the most obvious Christian duty to support the civil power in its struggle with heathenism. Sometimes the Church dignitaries became warriors, because the State had as much need of their swords as of their prayers. Nor is it necessary to conclude that the motive which drove them to buckle on their armour was base. When the Avars were at the gate a priest might be pardoned for leaving his oratory and joining battle. But the inevitable result followed in a deeper secularisation. Men were chosen to ecclesiastical office, not for their religious but for their secular prowess. That they had the capacity for affairs, or were strong men of their hands, became a reason why they were chosen to fulfil religious duties. And the men who were so chosen were compelled by circumstances to think most about that side of their work for their generation. What was an additional advantage in a Churchman became his chief qualification. Necessary it might be, inevitable in the circumstances of the time it certainly was. But, had it continued, the result would have been that the Church would have lost sight of its spiritual functions and that society, thinking only of the necessities of the hour and engrossed in present needs, would have failed to receive the stimulus and vivifying breath which only the Church of Christ, conscious of higher ends than those of the present hour, can give.

With the indomitable power of recovery and of returning for fresh inspiration to its Founder, which is one of the best proofs of the eternal power in Christianity, the tenth and eleventh centuries saw a revival of religion break across Europe. So soon as Christendom had won a clear space in which to pray and think, the Church returned to its specific task. There was abundance of work calling for attention. It had to recast its own thoughts about God and man. The brutalised manners which a long-continued state of war had brought on Christian Europe must be tempered by the spirit of the Crucified. The new strong-blooded nations which had found a lodgment within the Christian pale needed to be disciplined. Some of them were outwardly subdued. But, though Norman dukes and Danish earls accepted Christianity for themselves and forced its forms on their reluctant subjects, the conversion was only skin-deep. Even the princes did not greatly understand and could not heartily obey the faith they compelled their subjects to profess. Pagans, not merely in inward inclination but in outward practice, were found among the peasantry of Normandy for a century or two after Anselm had written his argument for the being of God in one of its convents. Because there was so much and so varied work to do, the revival of those centuries took several forms. It was as multiform as the life of which it taught its generation a new valuation. Three of the directions in which the deepened religious sense flowed need to be mentioned here, not because they were the most important, but because Anselm represented and helped to guide them.

As Churchmen grew conscious of having their own specific message, they realised how different in its aims the Church must be from any of the kingdoms of the earth, and how the qualifications which made men citizens of the nations were ill-fitted to make " fellow-citizens with the saints and of the household of God." The contrast between society as it is and society as Christ meant it to be can never cease to trouble the Church, if it is to be the salt of the earth. Every revival of religion makes that more troublesome. And the corruption of morals which had followed on long war, the deeper corruption which saps a society that has organised itself as a camp when the peril from without has ceased to threaten, drove the conviction of the contrast more sharply home to the conscience of the Church. A Puritanic movement with its cry of "Come out, and be ye separate" spread through Western Christendom. It took an old form common to both East and West, but new needs brought into it a new spirit. The form was that of monasticism. The monks were the Puritans of the early mediæval age. New monasteries sprang into being: Cluny, Clairvaux, Citeaux begin to be, and to be one of the most potent forces in Church and State alike. But though the form was old and in many respects familiar, the spirit was different. That most of the European monasteries accepted the rule of St. Benedict or framed new rules not unlike his great creation is in itself an indication of how new was the spirit which informed these foundations. The impelling motive was as before that men might save their souls alive, but they construed the method differently. They were not so entirely governed by the Manichæan conception of the flesh being itself evil, which in Eastern monkery lamed so much wholesome activity and, e.g., thrust into morbid prominence celibacy as the only form of chastity. Its presence cannot be denied. But it was no longer the controlling impulse in this revived monasticism. Rather was the fundamental impulse social. Men found themselves in a society which was based on war. So long as the war was waged against the infidel to keep Europe clear of paganism, the evil had been concealed. But when the threat of heathenism was withdrawn, the result it had produced on society remained. After heathen Norman and Dane had become outwardly Christian,

the princes and dukes turned against each other the
weapons the use of which they had learned to love
and the passions they had not learned to control.
Each wasted and ravaged the other's lands, slew or
led into captivity the other's vassals. With a dreary
monotony they passed from sacking a neighbour's
tower to repelling an assault on their own. And the
essential irreligion of it all became more manifest
when it was Christian men who thus fought with each
other. What had the Church to say to this state of
affairs? The Church might and did enter to check
excessive cruelty and to bid men show mercy after
the battle was over. But had the Church nothing to
say as to the constitution of society, which made such
things possible, and which made them seem to many
natural and inevitable? Many men in the disgust and
weariness which a society so constituted must bring
had looked back and seen the ideal of a society which
was based on love toward all men and on a consequent
peace. And, longing for it yet unable as matters then
stood to realise it, they went out of society altogether,
and strove to build up a society for themselves on a
new basis, the new and ever old basis of the obedience
to Christ. What drove them first was the need to
save their own souls and the recognition that while
they remained where they were they could not save
their souls alive. They became monks and more
particularly Benedictines, men who vowed themselves
to service rather than to destruction, to love rather
than to strife.

But this clearer vision on the part of the Church as
to its own specific purpose in the world had a further
result. So long as the distinction between the king-

doms of this world and the kingdom of Christ was not present to men's minds, there could be little conflict between the two institutions which represented these, and such conflict as did arise between Church and State could be determined by easy compromises which did not touch principles. But so soon as the Church grew conscious of how far its ideals were its own and came not from an earthly but a heavenly Master, it was sure to raise the question of ecclesiastical method. Every revival of religion must bring to the front the relations between Church and State. A Church which is conscious of its peculiar dignity and of its special ends will never be content to have its officials appointed and its policy dictated by men who must construe its purpose from a different standpoint. The conflict was certain; that it was so bitter was due to its novelty. While the efforts of the civil power were largely directed to keep Christendom from being submerged, the Empire maintained in men's imagination the sacrosanct character it had long borne. Its aims not unworthily represented the kingdom of God on earth. The Church, facing the immediate task and content to accept the State-ideal largely as its own, could well submit to have its methods of government controlled for such ends. While the bishops were State functionaries, and much of their energy was exhausted in fulfilling duties of a civil character, they might readily be appointed to office and even elected by the head whose work they aided. But when this temporary condition passed, and when Church officials realised anew their spiritual functions, they began to chafe, and the best among them to chafe most, against what now became an outside interference. The period

saw the long strife over investiture. The merit of
Hildebrand as an ecclesiastic is that he saw the issue
so clearly and clung steadily to one principle. He
struck at the centre of things when he claimed that
religious men—the college of cardinals, and neither
emperor nor king—must appoint the chief dignitary
of the Church. He wrought from the centre out when
he demanded that no archbishop should be consecrated
until he had received the pallium, the symbol of his
spiritual authority, from a pope so elected. He developed the system of legates who kept the several
national communions in close touch with the revived
centre of authority. He strove to break the custom
which had grown up of making Church dignities
hereditary property and the appanages of great
families by his canons against simony and in favour
of clerical celibacy. Certainly the old idea of the
superior sanctity of celibacy came to his aid, and he
used it unhesitatingly. High Churchmen have often
been heedless what heresy they helped to promote, if
only they could compass their immediate end. But
to him celibacy was not merely an end in itself; it
was the means through which he overthrew the
great ecclesiastical families and brought Church dignities under the control of the Church itself. It is
not difficult to see the evil results of much of this
policy and to recognise that it contained germs of
evil which were later to blossom rankly. The idea of
clerical celibacy brought a gross conception of the
religious life, which needed to be flung off in the
exaggerated protest of the Renaissance. The legates
continually interfering with the government of local
churches drew all initiative into the centre, until, over-

loaded with problems it was incompetent to answer and questions it could not understand, it simply ceased to act. The system which, at a time when the centre at Rome was full of fresh spiritual and moral life, sent life through every limb of the great body ecclesiastic made the corruption more swift and potent when the popes were Borgias. A means which religious men have used to promote a religious end often becomes a strangling cord round the neck of their less religious successors, who count themselves the inheritors of their fathers' purpose when they have only taken over their fathers' methods. But in its beginning the movement was the outcome of a new spiritual life within the Church itself. The more devout spirits welcomed it most heartily. The monks were Hildebrand's best supporters; the outcome of the religious revival, they recognised and furthered a movement which had its roots in the same soil.

And finally the deepened sense of religion produced a new interest in theology. Men had been fighting for several generations, they now began to think of the matters in defence of which they had unconsciously fought. Schools were founded. The monasteries began to copy the older literature and to write their own thoughts. The thirst for knowledge spread and drew men together. Hundreds of students flocked to Abelard's lectures. Men travelled across half Europe to have the opportunity of learning from Lanfranc. In these centuries the scholastic theology and philosophy had their birth.

And St. Anselm, as monk at Le Bec, as archbishop of Canterbury, as author of the *Monologium* and *Cur Deus Homo*, bore his part in this threefold movement.

He entered into it all, because he was a man of genius who was also a profoundly religious man.

And in no one man of the time is it possible to study its movement more purely than in him. The man dwelt with God. His work is the expression of that. It is not always possible to be sure about the cleanness of Hildebrand's hands. Not all the temptations of power nor all the greatness of the issues involved can excuse the inhumanity which Canossa proved to lurk in the pope, or expel the suspicion of an overweening pride. We confess to finding it difficult always to respect Bernard of Clairvaux, and his reiterated speech about humility makes the pride of the ascetic more open. One cannot entirely like Thomas à Becket. He leaves the impression of posing and of striving to live up to his part. Anselm leaves on one student of his lifework the impression of entire sincerity. He is one of the monks to whom the austerities and restraints of the convent have become a second nature. They have ceased to limit him, and consequently have become his support. The monk's cowl is part of himself. He stands up before William Rufus and Henry Beauclerk to fight the battle of the liberty of the Church in England. He fights it uncompromisingly, but through all his battle gives the impression of one who fought not for the interests of his order, but for what he believed to be the interests of the kingdom of heaven. He writes on the most abstruse questions with an extraordinary boldness, which the fact of his agreement with the opinions received by his Church should never conceal. Boldness in thought is too often claimed as the monopoly of the heterodox. In and through all his work the man stands as a wholesome man, answering with

what power he can, in the light of the strong religious
convictions he holds, the questions with which his time
brings him face to face. And so he has his reward.
For, whether men agree or disagree with the answers
he gave, they cannot fail to honour the spirit in which
he did his work, and must end by loving the clean-
souled, high-minded monk who, while seeking only to
serve his generation according to the will of God, has
made more clear to all after generations how that time
presented itself to the eyes and to the efforts of men
like himself.

# CHAPTER I

## THE VAL D'AOSTA

AOSTA, where Anselm was born between April 21 1033 and April 21 1034, lies on the Italian side of the passes of the St. Bernard. In its name, Augusta Prætoria, and in its ruined walls the town still bears the indelible marks of its foundation as a Roman settlement, from which one of Augustus' generals pacified the unruly tribes of the Alps. It became the centre of a deeper pacification when about the fifth century it was made the seat of a bishopric. And where the Roman Empire left walls, the Christian Church left the memory and the graves of saints. Unknown elsewhere, but remembered in the district to which their lives were given, the names of Saints Jucundus, Gratus, Ursus persist among the hills and valleys. Though his see was suffragan to that of Milan, the Bishop of Aosta seems to have maintained but a loose connection with his superior. Political rather than ecclesiastical considerations determined his allegiance, and he appears more frequently at the court of Burgundy than at that of his archbishop. The fact may have aided to prevent the little town from being drawn within the influence of the political and ecclesiastical ambitions of Aribert, the successor of

St. Ambrose, and to preserve it from the social upheaval which this prelate's restless spirit stirred up in his diocese.

Eadmer describes the valley as lying on the borders of Lombardy and Burgundy. In a period of uncertain frontiers to be on the borders of any state meant in every instance a shifting allegiance; and anyone who has tried to follow Burgundy through the early part of the Middle Ages will know how specially mutable that State was. But the Burgundy of our date was a county which Henry II. and Conrad had succeeded for a time in making an integral part of the emperor's dominions. And in 1034, after a fierce struggle between Odo of Champagne and Humbert the Whitehanded, the latter had brought the Val d'Aosta under his power. Anselm was therefore born a member of the German Empire and under the immediate rule of the Counts of Maurienne, from whom the present ruling house of Italy claim descent. But a border town Aosta was and had always been, set at one of the gates of Italy, with Lombards and Burgundians, Swiss and Italians thronging its narrow streets, with the peaks of the Alps and their walnut groves shutting it in on the north, while the Dora Baltea swept down beneath its bridge to the rich meadows of the Po. Anselm traced his lineage to the double strain in his people. Lombard on the father's side, Burgundian on the mother's, reared in a town which was too small to inspire a civic pride and had served too many masters to know a peculiar devotion to any, he may have found it easier to grow into a citizen of the kingdom of God, who was willing to serve his Master in Normandy or England as the need was.

In those days such a town and all Europe knew but two classes of society. And by birth Anselm belonged to the class which ruled. His father, Gundulf, and his mother, Ermenberga, were both members of the governing class to whose unquestioned prerogative we have no exact modern parallel. Both were *nobiliter nati*, gentle born, both possessed property, part of which their son could afterwards dedicate to the service of God. When the boy of Aosta had become famous as abbot and theologian, Humbert, successor to the Whitehanded in the county of Maurienne, was not unwilling to acknowledge himself to be of the same blood. A tower in the manor of Gressan, not far from the foot of the Becca di Nona, still bears the name of St. Anselm. The tradition may preserve to our time indication of the exact site of the property which Ermenberga is known to have possessed in the valley. And as the count had acquired fiefs in the same district through his wife who belonged to the house of Valais, it seems probable that Anselm's connection with that house was through his mother.[1] But the precise position held by the family in the social hierarchy cannot be clearly traced, nor, since it left little influence on the one member for whose sake the others are remembered at all, is it of great importance.

Gundulf is described as a lavish-handed, high-spirited man of the world, who was unwilling that through his only son becoming a monk his race should become extinct, but who himself took the cowl a short time before his death. He has perhaps suffered a little at the

---

[1] Rule has built up an elaborate pedigree of both Ermenberga and Gundulf. His conclusions are possible. Those interested in the matter may be referred to his book.

hands of Eadmer, since he belonged to a type the carnal valour of which no monk could quite appreciate. Yet his son may have owed something of his high courage and simple disdain of money to his Lombard father. Ermenberga was a careful housekeeper, striving to hold together what her husband was ready to squander, a pure-spirited woman, who looked well to the affairs of her own house and who found time to talk to her boy of the concerns of God's house. Her family had ecclesiastical connections, and this, when education was wholly in the hands of the Church, brought her son the best mental training which the time could give. Two of her brothers, Folcerad and Lambert, were *reverendi domini,* canons probably of St. Ours in the town. One of these was also Anselm's godfather, and to his charge as *nutritor* according to the custom of the time the boy was committed, that from this house he might attend school and be under the general supervision of his uncle. The school was in all probability in a priory which the Benedictine Abbey of Fructuaria had early in the century set up in Aosta. The Benedictines were already winning laurels in the cause of education, and doing what in them lay to answer the dawning mental curiosity of the century. Here, under the austere discipline of the age, the boy passed through the regular course of grammar, rhetoric, and dialectic. The monkish teaching fell on receptive soil. Anselm's Latinity, which is so sinewy and flexible as almost to read like his mother tongue, and his power of incisive analysis prove how honest was the work the Benedictines wrought in their priory among the Alps.

Of those boyish years we possess but few incidents. Yet the few which have come down serve to piece together some faint mental picture. One day Ermenberga received her son home and to her infinite distress hardly recognised him, so changed was he. While he had once been frank, he was now morose; he shrank from everyone's sight, and avoided even her caresses. The home with its larger interests, which should have charmed the schoolboy free from books and discipline, seemed to hurt him. He winced at its noise, found no interest in its activity, and sedulously avoided all its inmates. After the first pain of finding her child changed the mother-heart taught her the right cure—a little wholesome neglect. The boy, shy, thoughtful beyond his years, brought up without companions in the society of his elders, had been overtasked by his zealous tutors, who were doubtless proud of so apt a pupil, and whose methods both of physical and mental culture were severe even to men. He had been strained beyond his powers, and his nerves had given way. But there are only some lads who are capable of being overstrained in mental effort. Already his life-course was dawning in the boy.

Dreamy he was and full of the fair fancies which come to most children, but which persist in the thoughts of the solitary ones, and which, because they are not dislodged by the ideas of playmates, help to make the lonely souls. His mother had spoken to her boy, as mothers ever will, of heaven. And when the sunset burned among the Alps beside Aosta, the boy had seen behind its crimson and gold the palace walls of the Lord of Hosts. In his dream he set out to climb to it.

As he went he passed through the fields where women and men were busy at the harvest-work. These were the servants of the King, and, since they did their work sluggishly, he resolved when he had reached the presence to accuse them before their Lord. In the audience-chamber he found God seated on His throne with none about Him except the seneschal of His household because the others were busy in the fields. " So he entered, and the Lord called to him ; and he came near and sat down at His feet. And the Lord with gracious gentleness would know who he was and whence he came and what was his desire. He answered all according to the verity. So the Lord gave order, and the butler brought him bread of the whitest, and he ate and was refreshed in the presence of the King." Such was the story which Anselm, when archbishop of Canterbury, told the confessor who guided his private conscience, the secretary who helped him in his public duties. Among his childhood's thoughts this alone had persisted throughout his life. But there are dreams which at once betray and help to make men. And to the archbishop as to the child idleness was one of the great vices, and there was only hunger for soul and conscience except one had bread to eat which the world knew not of.

But the priory not only gave its pupil Latinity and guided him through the Trivium : it brought him into contact with the Benedictine order, and so with the rising religious movement which was giving the order new life, and which in turn the Benedictines were to do much to extend and guide. The boy was naturally religious, the whole atmosphere of his surroundings hitherto had borne the same character, his loneliness

2

had made the impressions deep. He was studious,
already so athirst for knowledge that he had worked
too hard. To his boyish thought idleness was a vice.
What was more natural than that the severe Benedictine rule should seem to offer the opportunity he
desired and to fulfil the ideal of a holy life? It
was true that his uncles were in the religious life
and yet were no monks. But canons in such a
place as Aosta were often little more than worthy
gentlemen of good family, whose birth gave them
admission to ecclesiastical posts which provided them
with modest revenues. On these they led respected
and respectable lives, and in return fulfilled certain
devout duties. When a new ideal of religious duty is
beginning to captivate men's minds, the representatives
of an older order are liable to seem destitute of any
ideal at all. A youth, above all in his early enthusiasm,
will count such a service of God insufficient, and in his
first ignorance of life will claim for himself a more
difficult self-denial. Anselm applied for admission to
a neighbouring convent. The abbot, however, refused
to accept him without his father's consent. Gundulf,
who had no mind to see his only male heir a monk,
refused his consent. The zealous boy — he was
about fifteen at the time—prayed for an illness which
might extort permission from his father. The illness
came, in answer Anselm believed to his prayer; but
the consent was still withheld, for it is difficult to force
the hand of the Almighty. When the illness had
passed, the desire for a conventual life had passed with
it. For some years he lived in his father's house and
forgot, as though they had never been, his earlier
desires. In later years the monk spoke with bitter

self-reproach of this period in his life as a time in which he plunged into excesses which left an enduring regret. But it is well to take self-accusations in such a man with a large reservation. To him, who had so lived himself into monkery that it seemed to him the only truly Christian life, the time during which he forsook his early desire seemed a time during which he forsook all religion. There may have been nothing worse in it than the wholesome reaction, when the lad rose from his bed and saw the green earth under him and the blue heaven over him, and filled his lungs with the Alpine air, and took back his life and his joy in the large world like a gift from out of God's hands.

About the year 1056 his mother died. She left besides Anselm only a daughter, Richera, to whom we find her brother writing in later years, and who was at the close of the century the mother of infant children. Richera must have been much younger than her brother, and it is possible that Ermenberga died at her birth. And when the mother was dead, father and son found themselves hopelessly misunderstanding each other. They had never possessed much in common ; and the strength of character which marked them both made them unable to cloak their difference. So long as the more spiritually minded woman had lived, she had kept the difference from rising to an open antipathy. Now, when she was dead, the situation became impossible. Gundulf was at no pains to hide his dislike. There was no one to soften it. Anselm at last could bear it no longer. He determined to leave home. In the early summer of the following year, with no very definite aim before him, he loaded his few necessities upon an ass and, accompanied by a

" clerk," crossed the Mont Cenis to disappear for three years in Burgundy and France. He went out not knowing whither he went. The instinct of his life was guiding him. Eadmer says he was not received into the convent near Aosta, because it pleased God that he should not be entangled in the conversation of the place. And certainly it was better for the world and for himself that he should profess, as he finally did, in Normandy rather than in the valley among the Alps. For in France was a religious and theological interest which no other part of the world could show. Italy and Germany were engrossed in the political and ecclesiastical side of the religious question. In Normandy Lanfranc was teaching. France was largely dominated by the congregation of Cluny, and with all its limitations, which were afterwards to make it the centre of Ultramontanism and obscurantism, Cluny was the most potent and pure ecclesiastical influence of the time. Eadmer might well declare it to have been of the Divine guidance that the future archbishop and theologian crossed the Mont Cenis.

# CHAPTER II

IN 1034 Herbert, bishop of Lisieux, dedicated to the Virgin-mother a humble Benedictine monastery not far from Brionne. Thither Anselm's unconscious feet were leading him when he crossed the Mont Cenis. In that brotherhood he should profess as monk, teach as prior, rule as abbot, before England claimed him. He should be one of the men who made Sainte Marie du Bec famous wherever good scholarship and holy living were valued. Since this became the " nest " to which in years of later trouble he looked back with longing, and since it gave him, perhaps the best, and certainly the happiest years of his life, it is necessary to attempt to recognise its significance for the Normandy of its time.

Normandy was in the making. The years of conquest were past. Already the great lines of its future strength were beginning to show dimly through the chaos. Yet the outward appearance of the land was no unfit sign of its inward life. It was still a wilderness of forest and swamp, where the clearings that should become cities stood out like islands in a sea. The townships were dotted here and there, grouped round a minster or a castle; and though the wooden houses were weak and the local institutions childlike in their simplicity, the cities of to-day often occupy the old sites and the civic life retains much from its beginnings. Above these, protector and terror, rose a Norman keep. Built less as a home than as a defence, its site agreed with its purpose. On some plain the encircling river was used to form a natural ditch; on a crag the walls were but needed to complete what the rock had begun, and the hand of time makes it difficult to-day to distinguish where Nature ceased and man began to build. Here a baron, as stark as the keep he had built, kept his own against his enemies and wrought his will on his defenceless tenants. He obeyed nothing higher than his own will, realised but fitfully that there was anything higher. "Every lord that was mighty of men made him strong, and many weened to have been king." Turbulent, lawless, loving battle, yet with fine elements of manly honour and knightly faith breaking through their brutality, these lived as they listed. Mortemer and Varaville had not yet taught them the strength in the hand of the tanner's grandson. So untamable were they that only the force of the Conqueror could restrain them and that the order which he had hardly maintained in his lifetime could not survive him. They could be bent by a more resolute will or outwitted by a clearer brain. But everything still depended on the individual ruler and his personal character. All the elements of a strong government in a young-spirited and intelligent race were present, but an ordered State was still to be built up.

The force which could alone moderate the baseness

as well as discipline the strength of the Norman character was still too largely a force from without. Christian they had been called for some generations. But their Christianity had been too much of a superstition to do much more than check their worst excesses and produce wild remorse of conscience, the cure of which was as superstitious as its cause. How little the temper of heathenism had died out among those Northmen betrayed itself when their still heathen countrymen burst into the country about the middle of the tenth century. Almost all the baptized fell back with relish into the practice of rites which they had not yet forgotten. Only those about Evreux stood fast to their new faith. Duke Richard I., himself too young to understand all that the step involved, was prevented by wiser counsellors from being carried away in the common apostasy. When he came to his strength he maintained the attitude which had been taken for him, won from his own people by his loyalty to Christianity the name *Sans peur*, and checked by his steadfastness the pagan reaction. And after he had with the help of neighbouring Christian princes made his duchy his own again, he set himself to revive monastic institutions there as the best means of renewing religious life. He restored convents which had been ruined, built and endowed new ones, gave every encouragement to the Benedictine revival among his people. Yet the canons of a council held at Rouen in 1050 show that paganism was still so much of a force in certain parts of the duchy almost a century later as to claim the attention of Church courts. What was able to survive even in outward form till then must have survived in spirit for many years later.

The fact, however, that the victory under Duke
Richard was won in the name of Christianity and
with one definite issue before it united with the
example set by the duke himself to produce in the
following century an outburst of ecclesiastical and
religious zeal in Normandy.  It was the period of its
great foundations.  " The abbeys of Jumièges, of
Conches, of Fécamp, of Mont St. Michel, of St. Wand-
rille at Fontanelle on the Seine near Rouen, of St.
Amand within, of Ste. Catherine or La Trinité du
Mont and St. Ouen without the walls of that famous
city, of Grestain near Lisieux, of Le Bec, Bernay,
and Cormeilles between Rouen and Lisieux, of St.
Evroult between L'Aigle and Argentan, of St. Leufroy
between Evreux and Gaillon, of St. Pierre sur Dives
near Troarn, were all restored, reformed, or founded
during the latter half of the tenth or the first half of
the eleventh century."

Yet, potent for good in the present and full of
promise for the future though these foundations were,
they long suffered under one fatal and common defect.
They did not belong to the people themselves.  Not
so much born out of their inward life as imposed upon
it from without, most of the monasteries remained
exotics.  Part of the stimulus to their foundation came
from political and dynastic considerations.  The rulers
had based their power on Christianity, because they
saw that there lay the promise of the future for
themselves and for their land.  They naturally sought to
strengthen the hold which religion had on their people's
lives.  They built and endowed, they encouraged
reform and brought in monks.  But religion needs
more than money and stones.  For years not merely

the ideals to guide their reformation but the men to carry it into effect needed to be drawn from among foreigners. The native clergy of Normandy were insensitive to anything except the outside of the movement, and the ideal of monasticism had not touched the conscience of the people. It is true that we only know the character of the generation from the records of their successors, who saw everything in the light of the later movement, and it is never safe to judge the morals and ideals of one generation by the new zeal of their followers. There were brave and holy men among the Moderates. But the complaints against the clergy of Normandy in those decades are too constant to be ignored. When Pope Leo IX. visited Rheims in 1049 the independent temper of the French clergy towards the Roman see without doubt made his judgment on their moral character more severe. The clergy who were not Ultramontanes were sure to find their marriage described as concubinage, their view on investiture condemned as simony. Yet that council found it necessary to pass a law forbidding clerics to wear military weapons or to engage in war. Many of the superior clergy chose the position not for the religious influence it offered but for the high position at court it opened. When the chief ecclesiastical dignity, the archbishopric of Rouen, was held during 113 years by three men, two of whom were bastards of the ducal house, one understands that there were disadvantages connected with the fostering care of the Norman lords. Men gave their countenance and their lands to the rising monasteries, but they still hesitated to give themselves. When they gave their sons, they gave these not so much to serve the aims as to enjoy the dignities of the Church.

The significance of the foundation at Le Bec is not to be found in its power to rival in dignity its contemporaries, nor in the commanding ability of its first abbot. In both these respects it was negligible. What gives it importance is that Herlwin in the prime of his strength elected to leave his knighthood and become a monk. The foundation represented the convictions of a man who gave more than a fostering and slightly patronising protection, because he gave himself. The Norman knighthood to their astonishment discovered that one of themselves counted their common life insufficient to satisfy the needs of his immortal soul and was resolved to rise up and seek a better. Now what those who are aliens to the common habits of a generation may choose to do does not trouble any generation greatly, it may even be put aside with an amused contempt. But when a man to whom life is offering the best which it can give to his equals gravely puts it away as inadequate, his deed strikes the imagination of the dullest. At last the ideals of monasticism had touched the Norman imagination, had reached within the Norman thought. One result was that the little house of religion exercised an influence quite out of proportion to its size or to the importance of its founder. And while it must be acknowledged that great part of its power is due to the circumstance that it was fortunate enough to count among its monks men like Lanfranc and Anselm, there must have been much of native vigour in the place, which could first attract men of such character within its walls and could then give them the opportunity they needed. The tales which have come down of the abbey's founder and his first illustrious monk serve alike to show what temper the men were of and the causes which drove men then into conventual life.

There lived at the court of Count Gilbert of Brionne a knight named Herlwin, one of the count's stoutest retainers. Sprung from a mixture of the Danish and Flemish stocks (his father Ansgot was of the old Danes, his mother Eloisa was akin to the Counts of Flanders), the knight was brave with the high courage which is more like hereditary instinct. He had been found wise in counsel and prudent in matters, so that his lord trusted him in the court no less than on the field. He was capable also of the generosity and quick sense of honour which can never be wanting in any man who is to lead men to a deeper understanding of the Divine generosity, without which in truth no man will ever see much in God to declare to men. Once his lord and he had quarrelled. The loosely-firm organisation of the period permitted a subordinate a large liberty in resenting any slight to his personal honour; and Herlwin judging himself insulted had withdrawn from Count Gilbert's following and was living privately at home. To him, sulking in his retirement, came the news that his lord had gone out to do battle with an old enemy, and that matters were likely to go hard with him, since the neighbour was stronger than he. The old loyalty awoke at once at the summons of the count's adversity, the temporary quarrel was forgotten, the slight to his personal dignity was disregarded. Herlwin gathered a troop of twenty men at arms, appeared on the very morning of the battle alongside his chief, and there—but not until with true Norman love of legality he had been reconciled in due form with his adversary—followed his lord to a victory his coming had made possible.

To this man, unembittered by failure and while his strength was still in him, the higher service of Jesus Christ revealed itself. He turned to listen, and as he listened, it grew ever more manifest to him that in this semi-barbarous society where war was alike the amusement and the business of his class, where he held his position and exercised his privileges on the simple condition of being ever ready for war, he could not truly follow Christ. Yet the rough soldier's wit could not but recognise the duties which his estate in life demanded from him. He could not flee from them. If he did, his superior would seize his lands and visit on his vassals the anger which he could not wreak on their now monkish lord. The man was in the strait to which the state of society must at that time have brought many a man who was determined to make earnest of Christian profession. For some time, since the count was obdurate and would not let him go, Herlwin tried to satisfy his conscience with subordinate sacrifices. He refused to eat the dainties at his lord's table and satisfied his hunger with the plainest fare. He denied himself the pomp of a warhorse, and where it was not possible to walk insisted on mounting an ass. The fashion of his utterance might be uncouth and awkward but cannot fail to appear of simplest truth. He was resolute to witness to the great reality which had become the one reality for him, that the obedience to Christ meant something more than the life which his companions in arms lived, and which himself had

lived until that time. The effort roused the amused
contempt of men who found it impossible to conceive
why a knight who was still sound in wind and limb
should even think of a monk's cowl. But this con-
temptuous amazement only made the weight of the
problem heavier on the solitary spirit. Herlwin bore
his false position as long as he might. At last it had
grown intolerable, and as often happens in such a case
an outward event served to transform into action a
half-formed purpose. He had followed his lord on one
of his unceasing raids into the territories of a neighbour. But on this occasion matters "fell not out to
Count Gilbert according to his desire. For Ingelram,
Count of Ponthieu, met him with a strong force, and
engaging him put him to flight with his men, and of the
fugitives many were taken and many slain and many
disabled with wounds. Then a certain soldier there
named Herlwin, fearing the danger and flying with all
his might for his life, vowed to God that if he got off
safe from so present a danger he would henceforth be
soldier to none but God." He escaped, and kept his
vow. No considerations could now hold him back.
Neither the threats nor the entreaties of the count
could prevent him from continually returning to his
plea for dismission. " By loving the world and obeying
you," so ran his petition to his lord in the words in
which a later age reproduced it, " I have until now too
much neglected God and myself: too intent on clothing
and too mindful of the body, I have forgotten the improvement of my soul. Therefore I entreat you to
allow me, if ever I have deserved well of you, to spend
my remaining days in monastic seclusion."

To a man who lived in that world life meant

obedience to other principles than those of Christ. So
soon as " it pleased God to reveal His Son in him," the
plain soldier had realised the fact. The sincerity of the
man's mind made him unable to shut it out. Custom
and familiar duties had retained him for a time,
even after his new-born conviction had made him
uneasy. It had needed the shock of outward circumstance to make his troubled thoughts pass into resolution. But once formed the resolution was irrevocable.
Only Herlwin had no thought of founding an institution, and just as little was he thinking primarily of
helping society. He was seeking to save his soul alive.
He craved to escape into an atmosphere which made it
possible for a man to think of self-devotion and to
practise self-sacrifice. It was inevitable in those days
that he should become a monk, almost as inevitable
that he should become a Benedictine. There was
nowhere else where he could go. For, whatever
they afterwards became under other influences, the
Benedictines were facing the question of their time.
Their answer was imperfect, as the answer of most men
is. But one thing they saw plainly and said fearlessly
at the cost of what most men value above everything
else, that society as then constituted in Normandy was
fundamentally unchristian, that so soon as a man made
earnest of his obedience to the great Master of all he
was bound to protest against it with what force was in
him, and that they for their part would protest by going
out from it and casting from them its rewards and
its hindrances. Therein lay the strength of this monasticism. It represented an ethical reformation. It
believed that Christ's principles were practicable and
were meant to be obeyed. And offering to earnest men

an opportunity for putting those into practice and the support of a society likeminded with themselves, it won some of the strongest natures to its service and its aims.

But the troubles of the new soldier of Christ were not at an end. He had but little knowledge of religious institutions. He could not even read. He looked about him for guidance, and found at first nothing but discouragement. In the courtyard of one monastery, where with all the embarrassed devotion of a new convert he stood silently watching the movements of the brothers, the porter mistook him for a thief, and having knocked him down from behind dragged him beyond the gates by the hair. On another occasion he was scandalised by the behaviour of the monks in their procession. Some were so busy displaying their Christmas vestments to the onlookers that they had no attention to give to their service. Two even fell to blows over their place in the ceremonial, and one of these finished the unseemly squabble by felling his neighbour. But the devotion which had resisted the sneers and the persuasions of the Count of Brionne's court was proof against the more difficult test of seeing Norman convent-life from the inside. He was cheered, too, it is said, by one simple incident. When he knelt in a certain church at prayer, a monk stole in alongside and all unwitting of a spectator prostrated himself to spend the long night in prayer and tears. But Herlwin would not enter into any of the religious houses which he knew; he resolved to found one for himself.

His first monastery was situated on his own property at Burneville, a few miles from Brionne, and was as humble a house of religion as existed in Normandy. Its heart and soul was the devout, indomitable spirit of its founder. Many of the stones of his first building were laid with his own hands. He taught himself to build. With his few companions, some of whom had been comrades in arms, he wielded mattock and spade. At the age of forty he taught himself to read, and as all the hours of the day were needed for more material cares, stole hours from his sleep to learn his psalter. The convent was miserably poor; sometimes the brethren had not enough to satisfy their humble wants. Herlwin consented to be appointed abbot in 1037, not because he desired the office, nor because he counted himself fit to fulfil its duties, but because no other could be found willing to accept the lowly honour. The site proved to have been ill chosen. Not even the diligent labour of the monks could make the wilderness yield enough for their maintenance, and there was no spring nearer than a mile or two from the building.

Some miles farther down its course the Risle is joined at Pont Authou by a tributary, which was too small to receive a distinctive name. Men called it Le Bec, the Danish name which still lingers in Cumberland for a streamlet. Here Herlwin elected to build anew, probably because he owned some property there. The rivulet drops down to the Risle through fir woods that furnished favourite hunting-grounds to the sport-loving Normans. After these had been in some way contented, the brethren removed to their new site and founded a convent which, like the old, they dedicated to the Virgin. Its fame made the brook famous: Sainte Marie du Bec, Our Lady of the Rivulet.

The number of the monks increased, and the spirit which animated them was excellent. Eloisa the abbot's mother, since she could help no otherwise, offered her services to wash the poor clothes of the brethren. But, though the abbot was zealous, he was also ignorant. Now zeal without knowledge will not hold a house of monks long together, especially when these are of the untamed Norman blood and many of them have worn a helmet before they put on the cowl. The discipline of Le Bec was suffering, and Herlwin had begun to feel keenly the want of the training which could enable him to guide the enlarging life of his little community, when circumstances threw in his way the man he needed. His sagacity made him fit to appreciate, his humility made him willing to use the gift.

Lanfranc, sprung from a legal family, learned especially in the canon law, with the instincts of a Churchman if not of a saint, had left his home at Pavia to visit France. Paris in that age occupied toward Rome the position which Alexandria held at a much earlier date as the school of a rising Christian theology and as the place to which every inquiring mind instinctively turned for light on the questions of speculation which were beginning to exert anew their perennial fascination on the minds of men. Lanfranc found his way to Avranches, and there taught for a time with profit and increasing fame. But teaching could not content him ; like many another he was looking with longing eyes towards a monastic life. As the story runs, he was on his way to Rouen to seek instruction in religion, when he fell into the hands of robbers. Thereon it occurred to the scholar how he

3

had heard of one in like case from whom robbers stole his horse and who proffered them the whip which was of no further use to him, with the result that the thieves touched to sudden remorse by his Christian patience restored their victim both horse and whip. Lanfranc thought to show a like gentleness in hope of a like reward and offered the men who had taken his goods his clothes as well. But, whether the Norman robber was coarser in fibre than his Italian fellow-rogue, or whether, as Lanfranc himself thought, Providence recognised and punished the insincerity of his offer, his assailants construed the request as a mockery, accepted the clothes, beat their wearer, and left him stripped and bound to a wayside tree. Here in equal danger of perishing from wild beasts and from cold Lanfranc sought relief in prayer. To his surprise and dismay the famous canon-lawyer and best Latinist of Europe found that in his hour of need he did not know how to pray. Lecture he could, but he could not even repeat a passage from his psalter. The incident determined him; and he vowed that if God delivered him from this peril he would instantly betake himself to a monastery and there before it was too late learn how to pray.

Some peasants found and freed him in the early morning. When he asked the way to the poorest monastery in the neighbourhood they directed him to Le Bec. In later years the gifts of the faithful made the abbey so rich that a doggerel Norman rhyme runs—

> "De quelque part que le vent vente
> L'Abbaye du Bec a rente."

But at this time the brethren could not from poverty

keep the light in their chapel burning day and night.
Arrived there, the new - comer was directed to the
abbot. He found Herlwin busy at the building of an
oven, half hidden in its rising wall. "God save you,"
said the Italian. "God bless you," answered the
Norman and added, struck no doubt by his visitor's
accent, "Are you a Lombard?" "I am." "And what
is it you would have from us?" "I would become a
monk." A brother was despatched to bring a book of
the rule. Lanfranc read it while the abbot went on
with his oven. Satisfied with its requirements, he
kneeled among the bricks to kiss his new superior's
feet. A few days later he made his profession as a
member of the brotherhood. And the quondam soldier
taught the great scholar and ecclesiastic how to pray.

As Lanfranc went in and out, a humble monk in the
humblest cloister of Normandy, he marvelled at the
things which he saw. For he saw a simple piety
building up uncultured men into nobleness of life, and
recognised how the sincerity and elevation of their
purpose cleared the men's minds of mists and gave
them direct insight into some spiritual realities.
Herlwin was so little of a scholar that he had needed
at the age of forty to teach himself to read. Yet
when he commented to his monks on Scripture and
tried in soldierly fashion to express the thoughts as
to God's purposes which St. Paul's Epistles awoke in
himself, Lanfranc wonderingly acknowledged how vital
his explanations were. He could not understand it,
he said, save that it was another proof of how the
Spirit like the wind bloweth where it listeth. And
the lawyer of Pavia who had lectured to the crowding
students at Avranches became like a little child, and

putting from him his pride strove to gain the best which the discipline of the cloister could bring him. One day, probably as he read to the brethren gathered to their midday meal, the abbot or another corrected a supposed false quantity in the reader's Latin and bade Lanfranc pronounce *docēre* what he had rightly called *docĕre*. He obeyed, and when asked his reason replied that he now counted it a greater thing to obey Christ than to follow even the grammarian Donatus.

On the other hand Herlwin was unwilling that this new brother should be buried among the ordinary convent-duties. He had not been sent of God to their monastery merely for his own sake but for theirs as well, and he could render them a service which they needed. Perhaps, too, the shrewd abbot who had not lived at the court of Gilbert without learning much about human nature knew how impossible it is for any man of real power to deny the nature which is in him. Lanfranc, associating only with untutored monks, having no one quite likeminded with himself, began to fret his heart out in morbid self-communings. He had even resolved and made preparation to flee into the wilderness and become a hermit. But the abbot, warned it was said by a vision, though it needed no larger vision than a genuine sympathy with other men can bring, showed such manifest distress that the other was softened to remain. Herlwin made him prior and brought through his more cultured nature a new tone into the little community. He encouraged him to resume his work of teaching, and when scholars, hearing that the Lanfranc whom they had counted dead was in Le Bec, swarmed to the place in numbers which embarrassed the monkish hospitality, Herlwin was willing to let the monks starve rather than the students. Among the rest came, drawn simply by the fame of a learning about which all Normandy spoke, another foreigner who combined the qualities which distinguished the abbot and prior of the monastery, who united the piety which distinguished the one with the scholarship which marked the other. Lanfranc brought Anselm to Le Bec, and for the sake of Anselm and of what he wrought there men still remember Le Bec.

# CHAPTER III

## Monk, Prior, and Abbot

THE Benedictines had from their beginning interested themselves in education. Prior to the ninth century, however, their schools were confined to the oblates, children dedicated to the monastic life and under training for that specific end. In the time of Charlemagne and doubtless through his influence the abbey schools had followed the example of the episcopal and opened their doors to all. Protest was raised by those who feared the secularising influence: a convention of abbots at Aix in 817 determined that the schools should be reserved for the oblates. But the large ideal of the emperor was too strong, and the result of the decision at Aix had been that two kinds of schools were instituted. There were now monastic schools proper, *scholæ claustrales*, where the boys were all virtually novices, and *scholæ canonicæ* which were open to the clergy and even to the sons of laymen. In some cases there existed within the abbey itself a training college where younger monks were put under a special director, either because they had professed without passing through one of the other schools, or because they were judged capable of benefiting from a further education.

38

When Anselm then appeared at Le Bec in the autumn of 1059, he came as a layman attracted by the fame of Lanfranc's scholarship. The religious impulse which had once made him desire to profess at Aosta was not dead but it was dormant. Nor was Lanfranc the man to reawaken it in a spirit like Anselm's. The two men were drawn powerfully to one another by the fact that they had in common many thoughts which they could only share with each other. The learned ecclesiastic could appreciate and guide the strenuous intelligence of his new pupil. The pupil never forgot his intellectual debt to his master. But, while they corresponded in later years on many subjects, their letters never show them opening their hearts to each other.

The spring of 1060 brought to Le Bec the news of Gundulf's death, and forced on Anselm the necessity of deciding what he meant to do with his life. He had already thought of becoming a monk. The scholar in a monastery fared as meagrely and slept as coldly as any monk in his cell. In many of its habits, in all its austerity the student's life was very near that of the professed monk. What it had not was the strength which comes from brotherhood in a common purpose and the hope of eternal reward. Why should he not take the vow which would require so little and give so much? Yet if he took the vow at Le Bec, he could be of little use there, since the abbey had no need of two theological teachers, and as the archbishop frankly confessed he was not then monk enough in spirit to relish the certainty of being eclipsed by Lanfranc. If, however, he went to Cluny the life of which he had learned during his wanderings, could his health endure

its austerities or would its monks be willing to use
the learning which he already knew must be the
master passion of his life? At times he meditated a
return to Aosta, there to devote life and patrimony to
the care of the poor. One thing only he was resolved
not to do, he would not live unto himself. Fearing
lest inclination should obscure duty, he asked the
advice of his prior. Lanfranc sent him to their diocesan, the Archbishop of Rouen; and Maurille decided
for Le Bec. It may have been the memory of this
decision, its hallowed results for himself and the
grounds on which it was formed, which gave a special
tone to his advice to an old pupil, Arnulf: "I highly
praise you, that you purpose going where you can live
according to your scheme, yet I warn that you do so
with the permission of your abbot, and that wherever
God direct your way . . . you choose no place where
you can be of use to and instruct others, but one
where you can profit from others and be taught by
them in the spiritual warfare."

Le Bec was under a modified form of the Benedictine rule. Entry into the novitiate was very
simple. In the chapter-house where the abbot presided the postulant prostrated himself, and to the
abbot inquiring his business answered, "I seek God's
mercy, your fellowship and the brotherhood of this
place: I long to become a monk and to serve God in
this monastery." The abbot replied with the larger
wish, "God grant you fellowship and a place among
His elect," to which the assembled chapter said Amen.
He then set before the postulant the duties and trials
of a monk under the rule. The postulant promised to
fulfil and bear them all. To this promise the abbot

answered, "Our Lord Jesus Christ so fulfil in you what for love of Him you promise that you may obtain His grace and life everlasting," and the monks again said Amen. "And we for love to Him grant what you so humbly and earnestly desire." After kissing the abbot's feet the novice was led to the church and there clothed in the dress and hood of the order. When the novitiate, which in Anselm's case must have been very brief, was past, the monks were assembled in the church-choir. At the close of the Gospel in Mass Anselm was led in by the master of novices. While he walked to the altar and prostrated himself on its steps, the Miserere was chanted by his new brethren. In the after silence the novice rose to read his vow from a slip of parchment: "I Anselm do before God and His saints promise the faithfulness of a monk, newness of life and obedience according to the rule of St. Benedict in this monastery which has been built to the glory of the blessed Mary ever virgin, in the presence of Herlwin its abbot." He laid the slip as an offering on the altar, and standing on its steps borrowed the words of an older ritual, "Uphold me, O Lord, according to Thy word and I shall live, and let me not be confounded in my hope." Three times this was repeated, and three times the monks, as though reminded of their own need by the hearing of another's prayer, echoed their new brother's petition. Then over the monk now prostrate the abbot intoned the De Profundis. A few prayers followed: the Veni Creator was sung: Anselm rising was sprinkled with holy water. His cowl was blessed by the abbot. His novice's tunic was removed — "The Lord put from thee the old man with his deeds." The cowl was put on him—"The Lord put on thee the new man who according to God is created in justice and holiness of truth." Anselm was a monk in Le Bec, and the kiss of peace was given him by his brethren. This was in 1060, when he was twenty-seven years old; and he was to live there as monk, prior, and abbot for thirty-three years.

Monasticism in the West had still the dew of its youth. To realise this, it is only necessary to see the three figures which are grouped round the rise of Le Bec: Herlwin, learning to read by night and building his oven by day; Lanfranc, the best Latinist and one of the sagest Churchmen of his day; Anselm, who pondered while his monks slept and whom the Church needed to summon on his obedience into the world of action. There could have been nothing stereotyped in a rule and a life which could attract and satisfy three minds of such divergent type. Regulations which would have been the breath of life to Herlwin would have stifled the powers of Anselm. But the fearlessness of a new enthusiasm was still present to the Benedictines. They were not afraid of individuality, within certain limitations they fostered it. Nor were they afraid of life. It was not a refuge the abbey offered, it was an opportunity. Every Benedictine community stood for one thing in Europe: it preached the sacred dignity of labour and the hatefulness of destruction. In an age when men counted their manhood by the amount they could destroy, when their pastime as their pride was to wreck or to prevent others from wrecking them, the rule which commanded labour as necessary to the soul's health reminded an astonished world of the dignity of labour. The monks in the days of their strength were the creators. Where others wasted, they built and ditched and taught. And the artisan and labourer dimly realised that these men brought him what all the sons of men must gain if their work is not to be a drudgery but a means of grace, the sense that their work also could in its measure be made divine. There were men too, like the Conqueror, who in that unquiet age only tore down that they might more surely rebuild. These were ever the readiest to acknowledge the help the Benedictines could lend them, and sought sometimes by hurtful privileges to foster their efforts or to purchase their aid.

The first three years in the convent were spent by Anselm in obscurity, the world forgetting, by the world forgot. But no sooner had Lanfranc been summoned by William of Normandy to become head of the monastery the duke had founded at Caen, than Anselm was promoted to the office of prior. Lanfranc had given fame to the little community so that men flocked to it for knowledge. It was felt that no one was better fitted to continue his work than his ablest pupil. But the first years of office were made bitter to the new prior. Envy is not abolished when its range has been narrowed. There were men in the convent who resented Anselm's rapid promotion, and who set themselves to thwart the man whose advance they could not prevent. It was only for a few years, for the simple purity of the prior's life, the high sweet dignity of his aims, the absence of all self-seeking, his invincible patience and almost womanly tenderness succeeded even in silencing envy. How much it cost and brought him is revealed in his letters. It is true that he never wrote about it. Indeed it is one characteristic of his letters that he rarely speaks about himself, and that while willing to help and counsel all who consulted him he seldom claims their guidance. Yet it is not without meaning that he so often urges patience on monks, and that the verse of Scripture which recurs oftenest is how tribulation worketh patience.

In the convent at the time was a young monk, Osbern, who though younger in years was older in religion than the new prior. His jealous seniors who dared not show too nakedly their own resentment encouraged the lad in disobedience to his superior. He set himself with the ability of a splenetic boy to worry Anselm in the thousand ways which the close relations of a small monastery make so easy and so wearing. The prior bore with all. Seeing a true heart beneath the monkey tricks, he resolved to win it, and to that end gave the lad special notice and allowed him certain indulgences. Slowly the ice melted. Osbern learned to believe in the affection of his superior and impetuously like a boy repaid it by an entire devotion. No sooner did Anselm see this than he altered his treatment. Little by little he withdrew the indulgences and began to test the youth's devotion by tasks which would serve to deepen it. Gradually the true character began to show more clearly. Already Anselm was able to rejoice in the prospect for his pupil of a nobler manhood which would be an ornament to the convent and a means to the glory of God. But Osbern fell ill with a mortal sickness. While the illness lasted the prior hardly left his bedside, and when the monk died, it was with the prior's hands ministering to his last necessities. Nor did death break that love.

Again and again in his letters does Anselm's affection for Osbern reappear. "Salute Dom. Osbern who is with you as my beloved brother for the dead Osbern, my well-beloved, . . . wherever Osbern is, his soul is my soul. During my lifetime I will claim on his behalf whatever I might after death hope from your kindness, so that after my death ye may be free (from the prayers for the dead). Farewell, my beloved, and to repay thee according to thine own importunity, I implore and implore and implore thee to remember me and forget not the soul of my beloved Osbern. And if I seem to burden thee overmuch, forget me and remember him."

Anselm's treatment of Osbern marks his power in education. The prior recognised what can be made of rich untutored natures by giving them an aim on which to expend their energy. While he recognised that strength which submits to no rule becomes weak or worse than weak, he had no monkish fear of vigour in itself. He believed in life and good and Christ: discipline and rule were but the means of attaining these more thoroughly. This eye for the foundations of character made him a revolutionary in educational method. The age believed in rigour especially in education. Guibert de Nogent mentions as a matter of course about his own, "meanwhile I was beaten almost daily with a cruel hail of stripes and blows." Monks in the chapter were beaten for slight offences. The oblates were taught to chastise each other when their masters had finished with them. To Le Bec came one day an abbot who opened his heart to his brother-educator as most men seem to have done who came in contact with the gentle prior. His lament was over his failure with the boys under his care.  We do our best for them, so ran his plaint.  We teach, correct, chastise them.  But they only grow worse: they learn no respect for us and, what is more grievous, no respect for the life to which we seek to introduce them: they grow up sour-hearted rebels: and I am well-nigh broken-hearted over the business.  Do you, answered the prior, pursue no other method than lashing?  See, brother, if you take a young tree with all its sap in it and check a branch here and tie in another there, what will you have a right to expect when you unbind the lashings?  Surely a twisted malformed thing which is good neither for timber nor for fuel.  And if you do nothing but check your lads, telling them they are wrong here, reminding them they are wrong there, can you wonder if all the branches of their natural capacity turn to gnarled worthlessness?  The homily was so pithy and so gentle that the abbot asked pardon for his mistake from his brother and from God.

Along with this went what is often bestowed on men who have forgotten themselves in a high purpose, the golden gift of understanding a brother's thought. Apart from the theological and historical value of the letters of the Church fathers they deserve examination as psychological studies.  The study is within a narrow range but is often extraordinarily keen.  Flashes of insight occur in Anselm's letters which prove his estimate not only of the value but of the dangers of the monastic life he strenuously followed.  Writing to Lanzo, an old pupil, he marks the disappointment many an ardent spirit must have suffered at the discovery of the cloister's drudgery.  "So soon as we have pledged ourselves to Christ's banner, the tempter comes to us not merely from without, he glides into the camp of Christ to ruin for us our service there. Nothing is more frequent than that young monks are tormented by scruples as to whether they have done right in becoming monks. Or though they will to remain monks, they imagine matters to be better in another cloister than in their own and ask whether they should not go thither. So they are like young trees which do not strike root in the new ground in which they are planted because winds move them hither and thither. Therefore your first care should be surrender to your new position, and it will not be hard for you to accommodate yourself thereto if you at first keep constantly before you the dangers which you have escaped, and thank God that He has suffered you to escape into the haven of the cloister-life, be it one haven or another."

The circle of Anselm's influence grew as his character became known. Men are quick to discover one who can give them help. Part of this was inevitable and natural as monks who had been trained under him went to other foundations. Lanfranc in his effort to reform the religious life of England brought over monks from his former convent. The men remembered their old master and turned to him with a sure conviction of finding unfailing sympathy. But others claimed help. From Hirsau the abbot who is trying to plant the aims of Cluny in the tough imperialistic soil of Germany asks guidance in a question of discipline. Some write for his books on metaphysics, others for copies of his *Meditations*, some make him their confessor in difficult passages of their lives, most beg for his prayers.

This increasing influence was due not merely to his
ripe intelligence but to the happy lovesome temper
which plays through his letters to his intimates.  He
seems to take a delight in forcing the monkish Latin
to express in ever-varying form his regard for men
like Maurice and Boso, his favourite pupils, or for
Gondulf of Rochester, his *alter ego*.  To one of these
who longs to be back at Le Bec but whom Lanfranc
needs and will not suffer to return he writes : " Although
the more I love thee, the more I could wish to have
thee with me, yet I love thee more for the very reason
which has separated us.  For since I love thee not
so much for my own sake as for the sake of God and
thyself, I love thee more, that thou provest thyself to
be such as that those with whom thou art are in no
wise to be brought to let go one who has won their love,
than I should, could they be readily brought to send
thee away.  I pray thee therefore as a brother and I
urge thee as a well-loved son with that care and diligence
which thou well knowest I have ever cherished toward
thee, that more and more thou advance in good conduct
and bear patiently with me our separation, so long as
Lanfranc orders it, counting it a divine appointment ;
and that thou in no wise by impatience lessen the very
ground of my greater love to thee.  For although I
deeply long that thou shouldest be with me in familiar talk, yet I more largely desire that thou shouldest
abide in good conduct."  And if he writes to his
intimates with tenderness, he writes to all his corre-
spondents with sympathy.  In all the correspondence
which has been preserved from the period in Le Bec
there is scarcely a letter which is entirely formal, or
which does not contain something of the writer's

personality. There is none which could give the correspondent the impression that he had intruded himself unwarrantably upon a busy man. The prior never wrote as though he grudged the labour. He gave himself to men who sought help and made them realise without words that he counted it a sacred and beautiful charge to be of use to them.

But these increasing duties pressed heavily on the prior's time and strength. The guidance of the schools was naturally in his hands; as naturally the correspondence of the convent fell to his care, for Herlwin was better with the trowel than with the pen. Again and again Anselm must excuse himself to the importunity of his friends for the brevity or the absence of his letters on the ground that he has not the time to write. The convent grew faster in the number of its monks than in the means for their support. It was still a poor foundation. Herlwin was eager to build a new church before he died. Anselm was resolute not to refuse the hospitality of the house to strangers or to the poor. Lanfranc sent generous supplies from England, but the prior wrote of one such gift that it had fallen like a shower on sand refreshing and evanescent, and of another that he and his monks were like Pharaoh's lean kine which devoured and remained lean. When the monks were hungry their superior bade them trust in God. They remembered in later years that they had never trusted in vain, but one suspects there were hungry days in Le Bec. The inward and outward management of a house of religion claimed gifts of administration which were not exactly at the command of the metaphysician. Once he sought relief from his diocesan and prayed to be allowed to demit his office. But Maurille who had sent him to Le Bec bade him go back and prepare, should God claim him for larger duties still, to submit to the claim.

Since the abbot was growing old and infirm his duties devolved more and more on the prior, and since the property of the monastery was increasing Anselm was often required to travel on the business of the house. It is said that Herlwin wished to give him for such journeys the necessary horses as his private property. But even at the words private property the monk felt a shudder of revolt. While he was still in the world, he had been impatient of the idea. " Even then," writes Eadmer, " reason taught him that all things in the world were created for the common good of men by the one Father of all, and that therefore according to the original ordering nothing belongs to one more than another." He would have joined St. Francis of Sales in speaking of sister Poverty. For the monks of those days embraced poverty, not merely because it implied a greater self-denial or freed them from the peril of administering wealth, but because they saw in it a means by which they could come nearer to their Lord. They had not forgotten how the Founder of Christianity elected poverty for Himself, and the way in which they construed human brotherhood made them the earliest socialists. This side of their action made of the early convents a potent social force. It is not only that a man like Anselm counted his revenues as abbot or as archbishop a trust which he held for God's poor. That was true, and it helps to explain part of the support which the commons gave to the Benedictines. But the mediæval peasant was degraded with a degradation to which we find no modern parallel. He belonged by birth to a class which could not hope to rise. His business was to cultivate lands which his lord would have counted it a dishonour to cultivate himself. Harried by his own superior to provide the sinews of an often un-righteous war, he was worse harried by his superior's enemies in order to destroy a source of revenue. If captured in war, it might be his fate to be butchered with his fellows in heaps because it was not worth the captor's while to hold them to ransom. And to his sur-prise, almost awe, he saw men some of whom belonged to the superior caste choose voluntarily an estate lower than his own in order that they might become better men. Not merely did the monk put from him some pleasures, the denial of which the peasant could not esti-mate. He denied himself warmth and food and drink the worth of which everyone could estimate. And men were helped to recognise anew that there are some things which contempt and poverty cannot destroy, to attain which the monk had deprived himself of what all men value. They saw anew the dignity of a manhood which counted itself rich so long as it could follow Christ, and which recked nothing lost so long as it might maintain its communion with the living God. The monks were preaching with the eloquence of deeds the dignity of manhood, which keeps its self-respect because it keeps its fellowship with the Eternal, and which does not set its greatness in the possession of outward things.

Anselm went back from his visit to the archbishop at Rouen to take up his duties sorrowfully enough. Nor had he long to wait before he learned the new burden which was to be laid on him; for when

Herlwin died in 1078, the monks assembled in chapter
unanimously elected their prior to the vacant office.
Anselm prayed them to have mercy on him. He
pleaded unfitness for the duty. They would not listen.
He flung himself on his face before them on the stone
pavement.   They answered his appeal by prostrating
themselves round the prostrate figure. Some of the
later biographers believe that the prior's reluctance
was due to the fact that the pope had recently formu-
lated strict orders against bishops and abbots accepting
investiture from laymen, and that the new abbot
foresaw trouble with his superior the Duke of Normandy.   But it was never Anselm's habit to surrender
a principle he had once accepted, and since the duke
never surrendered the right of investiture, this only
makes it difficult to account for Anselm's final consent.
The reason for refusal seems to have been much
simpler.   The abbey with its increased numbers and
influence required for its head a man with capacity
for affairs, and the abbot-elect was shrewd enough
in his self-judgment to know his unfitness.   When his
brethren insisted, however, his reluctance was overcome.
In February 1079 Anselm was consecrated to be abbot
by Gilbert, bishop of Evreux.

He had yielded out of that monastic obedience
which seemed to him the root of all virtue. But his
was not the type of mind which could interest itself
in many of the details which fell to the care of a
Norman abbot.   In the exercise of his office he was
required to sit as judge over the tenants of the abbey
property and to take his place as representative of the
monastery in some civil courts.   At these the love of
the Norman for litigation found full expression.   The

undeveloped code left room for delightful discussion on
minutiæ of procedure and justice. But men noted how
these things wearied the abbot of Le Bec and how,
when the wrangling grew hot over trifles, he leaned
back in his chair and fell asleep. They noted too how,
when the litigants had bewildered themselves hopelessly, the sleeper would often awake and show
a surprising power of brushing aside the heap of
sophistries and bringing men back to the heart of
the question.

These were not the matters which interested him.
But when men talked of some difficult passage in Holy
Writ or of some problem in theology they never found
their abbot asleep. To such subjects his mind naturally
reverted. They were his mental food. On them his
talk flowed easily and abundantly. Sometimes the
flow is too easy; the discussion is subtle but barren,
the light is a soft glow rather than a flash. He loved
to talk. Some of his parables, evidently the outcome of
daily life or wayside incidents, have been preserved by
his secretary, and many have the quaintness though
most lack the pungency of Luther's table-talk. With
his familiar friends the intercourse was very close.
There is a convent-idyl of the two friends, Gondulf,
afterwards bishop of Rochester, and Anselm: "They had
in God one heart and one soul, frequent talk on
spiritual things, much outpouring of tears during their
talk, mutual encouragement ever to climb higher, a
holy emulation to outstrip each other in God's work.
Yet Anselm as the more learned in Scripture was the
more frequent talker: Gondulf as the more liberal in
tears excelled the other in weeping. The one talked,
the other wept." The generous talker was accustomed

to complain that Gondulf was too eager to whet his knife at his brother's stone; but the talkers are rarely just in their estimate of the amount a good listener contributes to a conversation.

When the abbot visited a neighbouring convent, it became the habit to invite him to address the brethren assembled in the chapter-house. Some of his sermons have been preserved by the loving diligence of Eadmer. They have a character of their own. The speaker prelects rather than preaches. Gravely he elaborates, sometimes over-elaborates his points, driving them home by weight of argument rather than by appeal to the emotions. It is necessary to remember the audiences to which they were addressed, if one would really taste them. They were spoken to men who had already chosen their life-course and believed that in this troubled life they had found the one sure haven. Calmly they came together, the knight whose cowl replaced a helmet and whose feet rang no more on the pavement, the peasant who had left his plough to labour in the vineyard of God. They ranged themselves in the chapter-house, a group of earnest-eyed men to whom life had discovered its awe and who believed they had found its aim. They would listen to one who had better power than they to interpret their own thoughts to themselves and to make clear to them how their new life should be lived. And after this fashion the abbot of Le Bec spoke to them :—

"Amid other things weigh the miseries of this present life, and consider with how much care man must live among them. Consider that thou art fellow to him of whom Scripture saith 'man's way is hid, and God has surrounded him with darkness.' For in truth thou art surrounded by a deep blindness of ignorance, who knowest not how God weighs thy works, and what end thou shalt find thereto. Man knows not, saith Solomon, whether he be worthy of hate or love, but all things are kept secret to the end. Imagine that thou seest a valley, deep, dark, having all manner of torment in its depths. Conceive thereover a bridge, very long, yet of but a foot in breadth. Should any-one be compelled to cross this so narrow high and perilous bridge, whose eyes were bound that he could not see his steps, whose hands were tied behind his back that he could not feel his track with a stick— what fear and heart-sinking thinkest thou would he not realise? Would there be to him any room for joy or gladness, that I say not exultation? I trow not. All pride were done away, vain-glory were banished, the dark cloud of death alone would be turned over in the mind. Imagine further monsters of cruel birds flying round the bridge and seeking to drag down into the deeps that passenger. Should not fear be increased thereby? What if, even as he passed, the slabs should drop at his heels? Were not greater anxiety driven into him?

"Yet think over the parable and let thy mind be bound by divine fear. The valley is hell, immeasur-ably deep, dark with gloomy shadow. Thither flow together all miseries. There every softening influence is absent. All that can terrify and torment is present. The bridge perilous is this present life from which whosoever lives ill plunges into hell. The slabs which drop away are the days of life, which so pass by that they can never be re-lived, but as they vanish drive us on to the end. The birds are evil spirits, whose whole

desire it is to cast down men to hell. We are the
passengers, blind with the darkness of ignorance, bound
as with a heavy chain by the difficulty of a good life.
Consider therefore whether thou being in such peril
shouldest not cry with all thy heart to thy Maker, that
warded by His protection thou mayest cry in the crowds
of opposition, 'The Lord is my light and my salvation,
whom shall I fear?' Light, I say, against blindness,
salvation against difficulty. For these are the two
evils into which our first parent cast us, so that we see
neither whither we go nor what we should do, so that,
even when we partially see, being weighted with
difficulty we cannot fulfil what we rightly know.
Consider these things, O my soul, think of them, let
thy mind be daily exercised in them. Intent on these
recall thyself from thoughts of worthless things and
kindle with the fire of holy fear and blessed love to flee
from these evils and gain eternal good."

It is significant to remember the time in which
words like these were spoken by Anselm to his monks.
The contrast between the utterance and the circumstances in which it was spoken makes the strength
and weakness of monasticism more manifest. William
of Normandy and England was striving to curb
the disorder which his wanton invasion had caused.
Lanfranc was busy across the Channel with great
plans by which he hoped to quicken into new life
English religion. Hildebrand, long the master behind
the throne, had at last assumed the papal tiara as
Gregory vii. He had fulminated against simony and
denounced the marriage of the clergy. He had pro-
hibited lay investiture at the Roman Council of 1075.
He was offering bold defiance to the Saracen invader

in the South, and bolder defiance to the German
Emperor on the North.  He was striving to use the
Conqueror and the Normans in Italy for his schemes.
His own Rome had risen against him, and one wild
Christmas Eve had seen him dragged from the altar
across the city to a dungeon, only to go back after his
liberation and finish the interrupted Mass.  Henry had
deposed his adversary at the Council of Worms and
had been beaten to his knees.  Of these things Europe
was ringing, and men were wondering whereto they
would grow.  A new order was being born with many
travail-pangs.  So far as Anselm's correspondence
reveals, these and the like events might have been
happening in another century.  And it is not difficult to
understand how men bewildered in the storms of a
difficult time listened eagerly to the quiet voice which
called to them out of the convent and bade them
remember the inward victory without which nothing
was won.

Yet the abbot does not escape from the monkish
selfishness which spoils men who try to forget the
world.  There is a jarring note in a letter to Henry,
afterwards the head of Battle Abbey.  In it Anselm
bade Henry give up the idea of a journey to Italy,
though its purpose was to free his sister from bondage,
on the naked ground that the task would imperil his
own soul.  One is glad to know that Henry disobeyed.
Again he urged a certain William to leave war and
become a soldier of Jesus Christ and not be held back
from instant obedience by the vain hope of saving
his brother's soul.  The man had imbued himself so
thoroughly with the monastic life that not only had its
habits become a second nature, but no other life seemed

to contain any ideal of Christian service. These and similar letters prove how the system was producing its inevitable result even on this wholesome spirit. Fortunately for his soul's health the Church was soon to summon him back into the larger air of temptation and opportunity.

The man's real interest was in inward religion. There he was at home. If he turned away to consider other interests, it was because he must. The letters bear evidence to this. Not that he spoke much of experiences and feelings. The interest betrayed itself in a more natural form, in the high standard by which he judged all human endeavour and strove to test his own, in the lofty aims he sought to set before men, in the sincerity of his affection and in the perfect simplicity of his heart.

The inward flame of devotion which maintained his work burns most clearly in his so-called *Meditations*, which contain to our mind some of Anselm's best religious work. They are very unequal, variant in form, variant in matter, as a collection which had not the advantage of its author's revision could not fail to be. Here one finds the first sketch of the *Cur Deus Homo*, afterwards to be elaborated into a treatise. There one meets with exegetical studies which show an acute mind working with almost no critical apparatus. Again what begins as a meditation will pass into a prayer or rise into an act of adoration. But because his thought was so often busied with the misery and guilt of man and was so conscious of the limitations to all human knowledge, his piety has a chaste reverence even when it is most fervid. Because the thought of the merit of Christ and of Christ in His human life was his deepest comfort there does not appear the recoil from blank despair to morbid ecstasy which makes a great deal of the monastic devotion so difficult reading to those who have not been brought up in the same school. And there is an ethical strain in the work which gives virility to the most passionate devotion and which lifts it beyond the convent's narrow room so that it becomes universal in its appeal.

One lingers over this period, when the abbot was still in what he called his nest, before a larger duty and a more varied activity had called him to a wider field. It is not difficult to understand how a man with his affectionate nature and studious disposition must have looked back wistfully to a time which offered such scope to both. The convent itself remembered those days and adorned them with quaint tales, the grotesqueness of some of which cannot hide their beauty. They told how a sick brother, a bitter opponent of the prior, once disturbed the house, then in the peace of its midday siesta, with the cry that he was beset by two wolves which were attempting to throttle him. Instinctively men ran for the prior whom they found correcting his beloved manuscripts in the cloister. It needed but that he should make the sign of the cross in the doorway of the infirmary for the sick monk to see a flame dart from his lips and put the wolves to flight. Again, one who went about nightly duties in the convent and roused the monks to their office saw the abbot kneeling at his private prayers in the chapter-house, and his head was encircled with flame. Wondering whether all he saw was a vision, the monk stole up to his superior's room only to find it empty. They told again how the abbot with a few monks once arrived at the house of Walter Tirrel. As the visit had been unexpected their host was unprepared and the provision at table ran short. Tirrel abounded in apologies, but Anselm bade him not give himself any trouble because provision was even then on its way to the castle. And in truth a servant arrived soon after, and brought with him a sturgeon which of course was the largest that had been taken in the district for many years.

We have fortunately reached a stage at which such tales can be read without anger or contempt. In an age which in nowise vexed itself about the difference between the fixed laws of Nature and the direct interference of God, men recognised that this man stood nearer the Almighty Source of all strength and good than themselves, and they uttered their conviction in the way which appealed to their minds. Anselm's sanctity, his resolute patience, his self-abnegation, his simple confidence in the will of God, his inability not to help other men, were so manifest that they won to uttermost reverence the hearts of the rude Normans who came to Le Bec that they might find God, and who, as most men do, found Him mediated to them through the word and life of one who was at once so like and so unlike themselves.

# CHAPTER IV

## THE MONOLOGIUM AND PROSLOGIUM

THE first of the writings which make Anselm recognised as the leader of a new movement in thought were produced when he was prior and abbot at Le Bec. Like most of his other work this came to seek him rather than needed to be sought by him. Several of the younger men who had received their theological training in the Norman monastery felt the difference between their early tutor's method and that of the few books to which they had access. From the convents, for the service of which his training had fitted them, they wrote to request copies of the lectures which had roused their minds to think. Reluctantly the abbot consented, but for a time persisted in sending out his writings anonymously. Only when he found how easily errors multiplied, did he consent to attach his name to authoritative copies. Perhaps, too, the claim of the heretic Roscelin that the famous teacher of Le Bec agreed with his views on the doctrine of the Trinity helped to discover how a false humility brings perils with it, and made Anselm more willing to declare his actual opinions.

Europe was beginning to awake from its intellectual sleep. The minds of men were stirring to inquire into the dogmas they had long been content to accept. There was a joyous confidence in the way they flung themselves on the world-old problems. They had yet to learn the limitations of their powers. And Anselm delighted in his task of education. His power lay in quickening the intelligence of the youths who were committed to his care. The mind of young men, he was accustomed to say, is like wax which is of the right consistence to receive and to retain the impression which one wishes to make on it. The mind of children is too fluid, easier to impress but more impatient to retain the impression. The mind of old men has so hardened that it keeps all it has once received but refuses to accept anything new. Yet the abbot was not unaware that part of his preference for such students was due to his own inability to give the teaching which younger children need. In a letter to one of his favourite pupils, who was then probably acting as secretary to Lanfranc in England, he expressed the pleasure it gave him to hear that Maurice was using the opportunity to benefit from the instruction of a famous grammarian, Arnulf. "You know how I was always weak in declinatio, and incapable of labouring with you in the minutiæ of grammar." His mind was not that of the exact scholar, it was interested in principles rather than nice exactness of detail. Of anything which did not relate itself to a principle he was soon weary. His power lay in rousing and guiding minds which were beginning to feel out after such principles.

The method of education prevalent in the monasteries of the time helped a real thinker to impress his personality upon his students, and the fact that the school at Le Bec was new gave its founders a freer hand.

Books were then a rare and costly luxury. All the chroniclers unite in praising the library at Le Bec. But an exact catalogue of its contents at least a generation later than Lanfranc's priorate has been preserved, and it makes the modern reader wonder what poverty was, if this was counted riches. The list contains the names of forty authors of whom more than three-fourths are ecclesiastical. Even copies of Holy Scripture must have been difficult to procure, for, when Archbishop Lanfranc wrote to request the convent copy of St. Paul's Epistles, Anselm sent it with a very visible reluctance and only "in obedience to his orders." Such books as were to be had had been transcribed by the monks. An illiterate age did not merely write nothing of its own but was careless about the correct copying of older works. The manuscripts were crammed with errors. Long into the night by the flickering and scanty light of a candle the prior sat busy with the toil of transcription and with the more laborious toil of collating and correcting his volumes. Again and again in his letters appear petitions for books of all kinds. The Rule of St. Dunstan, the Epistles of St. Paul, the Aphorisms of Hippocrates—they form a curious medley. But especially does he beg that the copies made and sent to him should be accurate. "Send me a copy of the Aphorisms. If you are unable to copy it all, copy a part. But above all send it me without errors. I would rather have a part correctly copied than the whole crammed with mistakes."

In this dearth of books the convent teachers were thrown back on the Socratic method of question and answer which is easy only in appearance, and which

when honestly and fearlessly used is the surest means
of attaining clarity of thought. That Anselm preserved the form in some of his published works (the
*Cur Deus Homo* is written throughout in the form of
a dialogue) is the proof of how he had used and valued
the method in practice. Occasionally the dialogues
do not escape from the peculiar vice of the method,
especially when it is employed within such surroundings as a convent affords, the vice of pursuing a
principle into needless minutiæ. The convent school
and the synagogue school have many things in common. And often one is conscious of the atmosphere
which easily steals into the minds of men who having
shut themselves off from the world's larger interests
come to believe that a logical definition determines
everything and forget that the world is not governed
by the rules of Aristotle. But at least the teacher if
he could think himself had the opportunity of laying
himself alongside the minds of his students and of
encouraging them to test his results. The method
was even more fruitful than its results could be. It
quickened thought. Before Anselm's day theologians
were content to quote, and a citation from St. Augustine
was sufficient to decide a question : after his day they
began anew to think for themselves.

A contemporary declares with just a touch of envy
or of contempt in his tone that all the monks of Le
Bec were philosophers. And as scholars spread abroad
from the Norman school, one cannot help suspecting
that their teacher was shrewd enough in his judgment
of human nature to dread sending into the monkish
world a set of theological prigs who might disdain the
simpler piety of other convents and look contempt-

uously on men who were nearer God than they because these simple monks could not reason according to the schools. Their old master was too loyal to them and their common mission not to point out the danger. It is not difficult to read between the lines of a letter written to a pupil in answer to one in which the monk had expressed the wish to leave his present convent, because it did not offer scope enough for his intellectual powers. Very gently but firmly Anselm bade him remember that he might also consider the advantage of finding a place in which he should have opportunity to learn, and that the very place in which he then was might offer the opportunities he needed.

The surest preservative, however, against the vagaries of such men was the influence of their teacher's profoundly religious spirit. With Anselm exact thought on the mysteries of God and His relations to the world and to men is not pursued as an intellectual satisfaction nor regarded as an end in itself. It is the means toward the larger end of setting the spirit into right relations to its Source and Father. Metaphysician though he was, with a bent toward the severest thought on the most difficult subjects, delighting in the exercise of his own disciplined intellect, his instincts were religious. This appears even in the form of the *Proslogium*. When he has, as he believes, established the proof of God's existence, he breaks out into an ascription of praise which has a lyric note in it, because God has thus revealed Himself to one of His creatures. Only this is rare. Anselm did not turn aside, like many Romanist and Evangelical theologians, to interlard his severer thoughts with devout expressions. He did not feel the need to turn

5

aside. To him thought on God, His attributes, His
will, was an act of piety. And in a manner peculiar
to himself he has succeeded in saturating many of
his austerest discussions with his own devout temper.
On the other hand the genuine thought and high
ethical purpose which inform all his devotional writings have helped to give them endurance. The prayers
and meditations of the prior of Le Bec were in constant use through the Middle Age. Any mediæval
collection of devotional literature is sure to contain
several of Anselm's compositions.

Alongside of this devotion went a confidence in the
power and validity of human thought which lends an
extraordinary boldness to much of his speculation.
Anselm is no rationalist in the usual sense of the
word. There are some truths which it is beyond the
human intellect to comprehend, and to which though
it finds itself unable to comprehend them it must still
bow. How these are mediated to men and what is
the ground on which they must be received he does
not stop to inquire. That they were contained in
Holy Scripture and in the Creeds of the Church
would have seemed a sufficient answer. Men had not
the historical and critical knowledge which raised
both questions. To Anselm the Church's dogma was
divine in its origin and in its authority. But human
intelligence was equally divine in its origin, and within
limits in its authority also. The truth which is received by faith and the truth which is discovered by
intelligence are both of God. They cannot finally
conflict, simply because they come from the same
Source. Should they appear to conflict, as they
often do appear, the devout must hold by faith,

though he need not surrender the effort to attain to the reconciliation. *Credo ut intelligam* ("I believe that I may understand") is his unhesitating avowal. This position sets the monk very far from the attitude *credo quia absurdum* ("I believe because it is incapable of being understood"). That was sometimes the refuge of scepticism, sometimes the defiance of ignorance. Anselm was no sceptic. All things in the universe were only real so far as they were the outcome of God. As man's mind was the crown of God's world, human thought was capable of attaining a real and valid knowledge of eternal things. Yet the position so stated proves no less clearly that this devout Churchman had been vexed by questions he was unable to answer and doubts he was incompetent to solve. The dogmas of the Church did not possess to him—and what he was able to express was being dimly felt by an increasing number — that power of self-evidence which rendered them independent of any outward support. Men felt, and Anselm among the rest, that they needed some support. Scholasticism was the attempt to supply it.

The *Monologium*, or, according to its subtitle, Faith seeking Understanding, is a meditation of the soul on God. It attempts, putting aside all Scripture authority, to prove the being of God in the light of pure reason, and then to define His nature and attributes, His relation to the world and men. The book begins with a proof of God's being as implicit in ordinary experience. All things which are must have a cause. What a man desires at any particular moment is some good, something which has intrinsic value or only supposed advantage. But all these particular goods must have a common origin in some original good. So is it with everything which rouses man's reverence. What quickens such reverence proves the existence of some original sublime. Anselm labours and elaborates this statement and then argues that all particular beings must have their origin in what is either manifold or one. To think of the final cause as manifold is to end in hopeless contradiction. Reciprocal dependence which were one solution is an absurdity. And entire equality of those manifold final causes would inevitably, if it were carried to its issue, imply essential unity. There is then but one final cause which is God, who Himself is at once self-caused and the cause without which nothing else can exist. God owes His being to none other than Himself; all other existences in the universe owe not only their being but their continuance to His necessary being.

And the unity of God is absolute. His attributes cannot be distinct from Himself, nor yet can His unity be one which is made up of parts. For that which is made up of parts, or which has attributes that can be thought as distinct from itself, is conditioned by its parts or by its attributes. But God is unconditioned. He has therefore no parts, and His attributes are but methods by which we name His being. He cannot be said to have truth, and even to say that He is true is to run the risk of limiting His simple and immutable being.

How then did the universe of contingent appearance come to be, and how can it be thought in relation to God? There is but one method, the creation out of nothing by the fiat of God. In his teaching about creation Anselm follows Augustine closely except that he adds certain Platonic elements to the great African's doctrine. The creation out of nothing involves beginning in time. There was then a time before which the universe of created things had no existence by itself. But this does not imply that it had no existence whatever. In a sense it existed from the beginning. It existed in God's thought even before all time. That God saw that the universe would come into being, that God not only foresaw its actual existence but had even predetermined its coming into existence constituted for the universe an eternal existence. In this sense it *was* before it *became*. Anselm does not succeed any more than many another in avoiding Pantheism in his representation of God's relation to the world of contingent things. That is due to his profound conviction of the essential unreality of all things without God. The world possesses reality only so far as it expresses spiritual truths and embodies spiritual relations, the source and explanation of which is God. The same conviction is also the foundation and the truth of his ontological argument. The relative implies the absolute, or else itself has no reality. No theologian who has ever been possessed by that conviction and has tried to give it utterance has escaped the lapse into Pantheistic modes of expression.

There follows a discussion on God's nature, and first on His attributes. This moves on familiar lines; but one thing is noteworthy in it. Anselm's strongly monistic position which led him to emphasise with special force the simplicity and immutability of the divine nature causes him peculiar difficulty when he has to discuss omnipresence and eternity. Because of His undivided

unity of essence God cannot be omnipresent in the
sense that He is distributed in all places and at all
times. Omnipresence can only mean that the divine
undivided essence is at once in every moment of time
and at every point of space. So it is with eternity.
God is everlastingly. Anselm states the conclusions to
which his rigid logic has driven him, but does not hide
from himself how largely meaningless or how largely
symbolic such words as essence and substance, space
and time must be when applied to the Absolute.

The second great section dealing with God's nature
is occupied with a discussion of the Trinity. On
this subject the monk had evidently brooded long.
The question was rousing new interest in the Church,
which in the confidence of its long untried powers
of speculation ventured to discuss the highest subjects. Roscelin was teaching what was counted
heresy. Anselm puts out his whole strength when
he deals with it. "The Word is the object of eternal
thought: it is God in so far as He is thought
conceived or comprehended by Himself. The Holy
Spirit is the love of God for the Word and of the
Word for God, the love which God bears Himself."
In general the Church in the discussion of this high
subject has varied between a position which insisted
on the distinction of the "persons" to the neglect of
the essential unity, and one which in the fear of
verging on Tritheism has emphasised unduly the
unity of the divine nature. Anselm's whole discussion
leaves the impression that he has not escaped the
latter. It is difficult to distinguish his Word and
Spirit from modes of the divine activity.

After the *Monologium* was written, however, its

author was not satisfied with the part of his work which was concerned with the argument for the being of God. He sought one single argument which might establish that at once. Probably the monk's acute intelligence, which was not destitute of a touch of scepticism, had suggested to him that it was possible to decline the step on which everything was based. The empiricist might decline to go beyond phenomena, might question the existence of anything beyond them, might suggest that the supposed reality behind them was nothing more than an idea. Nominalism was not yet full-blown; but what gains full expression in a later generation is often felt already by an earlier.

The thought of a single proof for God's existence troubled the philosopher-monk. It would not suffer him to sleep, and made him even more careless than usual about his meals. It hovered between him and the manuscripts which he corrected. Even the common prayer became at times a routine duty, while his real thoughts followed the elusive phantom. So commanding did it grow that the man wondered whether it might not be a temptation of the devil, and tried to put it away from his thoughts as such. But everything was in vain. At last, after many painful days and troubled nights, the idea which he had pursued so long came to him during vigil. Hastily, lest the idea should escape as swiftly as it had come, he seized his tablets and committed a rough sketch of the argument to the wax. But an evil fate pursued the work. The monk to whom the sketch was entrusted lost it, and a second copy suffered as evil a fate. The brother to whom this tablet was delivered hid the precious trust in his bed, only to find it dashed in fragments along the dormitory floor. The fragments were pieced together and from them Anselm wrote out on parchment his famous argument for the being of God. He cast this in the syllogistic form so loved of the Schoolmen, a form which was incompetent to express thoughts of that type. The very hardness of the form may have helped in later years to conceal the meaning of the idea.

Scripture, so the *Proslogium* urges, is right when it calls him who denies God's being a fool, for his very denial implies a self-contradiction. He stultifies himself by the statement though he may not realise the fact. The man has in his mind the thought of the highest of all beings, than which none greater can be conceived. The idea of this "highest thinkable" is in his mind, since it is thinkable. But this highest thinkable must exist not only in the mind but also in reality. If it do not exist in reality, there must be something higher than it which can be thought, for that which has actual existence is higher than that which does not exist otherwise than in thought. That is, the thought is not really the highest thinkable. Let the idea then be really the highest thinkable, and it must exist in fact as well as in the mind.

Further, contingent existence is lower than necessary existence. If then the highest thinkable exists in fact, it must also exist necessarily, alike in thought and in fact. This has the idea of God, at least contains enough of the idea of God to prove that he was indeed a fool who denied His existence.

The argument was no sooner published than it roused opposition. Gaunilo, a monk in the neighbouring convent of Marmoutier, entered the lists with an apology for the fool. An illustration from the monk's pamphlet is more familiar than the general bearing of his argument. "Some say that somewhere in the ocean is an island, which from the difficulty or rather impossibility of discovering it (since it does not exist) they call the Lost Island, whereof they fable much more than of the Isles of the Blest concerning the inestimable fecundity in natural resources and all manner of desirable things by which it excels whatever lands men till. I may hear of that island and understand what I hear, but if my informant were to add, 'Now you cannot doubt that such an island exists somewhere in fact as well as in your mind, because to exist in fact is more excellent than to exist in imagination, and if it did not really exist any land which does would be more excellent than it,' I should either think he jested or be at a loss to say whether he or I were the more silly." The analogy was an imperfect one, nor had Anselm much difficulty in pointing out the fact. But the real edge of Gaunilo's attack was not so easily turned, nor does it seem to be turned in his opponent's reply. The monk of Marmoutier wrote so obscure a monkish Latin that any conception of his meaning is offered with considerable hesitation. He lays his finger on the ambiguity about having a certain thought in the mind. Widen the content of that or any other thought as much as you please, you have not succeeded in making it any more than a thought. You cannot thereby confer on it objective reality. Its existence is certain, but only its existence as thought. Men can pass from thought to thought, from existence to existence, but not from thought to existence. To add to the content of thought does no

more in the end than add to *thought*.   What finally is
secured by Anselm's argument is the existence of the
God-idea.   But that of the existence of which the
theologian desires to be convinced is the personal
Deity.

This is not the place even to attempt a discussion of
the final value of this position, but one fundamental
characteristic of Anselm's two books on the existence
of God deserves notice.   They mark the first real
effort in Western theology to reach a surer foundation than Augustine offered.   Augustine, who until
this time had dominated all the theology of the Western
Church, a citation from whom was sufficient to close
discussion, never overcame the dualism of his Manichæan training.   Anselm is impatient of all dualism.
He is never content till he has transcended it.   Hence
sin has to him no positive existence, but is a mere
negation.   His conception of the Trinity runs the
risk of sacrificing the distinctions of the three persons
to their essential unity.   The created universe has no
reality save so far as it embodies some word or purpose
of God, and his doctrine of creation comes perilously
near to Pantheism.   He boldly denies the hard distinction between thought and being.

All these may be counted heresies in theology and
philosophy, or if not full-blown heresies at least the
buds of error.   But the work of Anselm helped to
bring the idea of God's immanence into clearer place
in the Church's theology.   God was in and through
His whole creation.   Without Him the world could
have no reality.   And the crown of all the world was
man, who as rational and self-conscious was the highest
expression of the divine purpose.   Not only is it man's

duty to seek and serve his Creator, it is also possible to him because God and he are not far off. Inadequate therefore man's thoughts may be; when concerned with God and His nature, inadequate they must be, because they are human. But true within their limitations man's thoughts must as surely be, because God has been in them. There is in Anselm nothing of the latent scepticism about the validity of human thought which lurks in so much of the later Roman and mediæval theology. Faith was the gift of God, but intelligence was no less the sign of His indwelling presence. The two could not finally conflict.

And is it not this which lies at the foundation of the *Proslogium*? State the argument as a syllogism and with Scotus Erigena it will always be easy to point out how the conclusion is subsumed in the premiss. But the finite has no reality apart from the infinite. The relative and contingent imply the absolute and necessary. Unless we deny in any real sense of the word the existence of the finite human spirit, we must accept the existence of an infinite spirit. If men are not to be shut up to absolute Pyrrhonism, they must make the leap somewhere. Anselm made it with the utmost boldness. It is quite easy and interesting to argue that the existence of all things including man is no more than a passing shadow, because the only ground we have for holding the opposite is rational necessity. But, when a man holds this conviction, he has ceased to think rationally. Anselm would apply to him the scriptural epithet.

# CHAPTER V

## THE CHURCH IN ENGLAND

THE period of comparative retirement in the monastery was soon to come to an end for Anselm. The world on which the man had turned his back in order to find God in solitude claimed the fugitive. So it chanced again and again in that age of violent and picturesque contrasts. Though the barons were coarse, though their religion often deserved no higher name than superstition, they recognised in the monks the note of moral earnestness which to the ignorant seems to be everything. In straits they turned to the convents for their confessors, and often for their bishops. To the monks they gave the charge over their souls, disobeyed them, fretted against their authority, were awed by finding the powerlessness of vulgar threats against their resolution, and were leavened unconsciously by their principles. Many a monk in such circumstances may well have been perplexed, as Anselm's letters prove him to have been, by the difficulty of reconciling his purpose as a monk with his work as an ecclesiastic. The desire to renounce the world was a divine inspiration: the summons to govern the Church and thus return to the world was no less certainly a call from God. And as humble men must do, they solved the contradiction by obedience and learned to distrust their own desires. Many who were as unselfish in spirit as the abbot of Le Bec learned from the contradiction to see their new dignity in the light of a trial and to wear the bishop's mitre as a test of their Christian character.

The Church, when she was gathering all her strength to the fight with what is called feudalism and to the assertion of a kingdom which is not of this world, could not afford to leave a man like Anselm in the peace of his convent. Such a man was a weapon tempered to her purpose. Ill equipped though he might be for the struggle by the habits of his thought, he was splendidly equipped by the habits of his life. His was rather the skill which knows how to resist than that which is capable of attacking. He might be incapable of arriving at a solution which, like most working solutions between two great living forces, was sure to take the form of a compromise. His mind was too dogmatic for any compromise. But he was equally incapable of betraying a principle he had once maintained. The methods of the practical Churchman were foreign to him, the methods of one who is content to secure the admission of a principle under an apparent concession, and who can afford to leave time to work for his cause in bringing the principle to its inevitable development. The monk had a blunt habit of stating his whole thought with all that it implied. To him the admission of the germ involved the acceptance of the conclusion; and he stated the conclusion. He really believed that average men are governed by reason, and thought that logic has a great deal to do with the management of affairs.

His excuse must be that he had lived in the cloister, and even there had had his closest association with men who came to him seeking after truth. He had not had the opportunity to learn how largely self-interest and prejudice govern men even in connection with ecclesiastical affairs. On the other hand, and therein lay his strength for the Church, when he had once taken up his position, he was immovable. Nothing but the proof of his being in the wrong could stir him from his place. It does not seem to have occurred to him that it was possible to betray a conviction for the sake of ease or personal advantage. An age when great principles were being fought out needed such men.

It is necessary to go back in the matter of time in order to show how the opportunity which was to widen Anselm's sphere of activity came to him, and what were the circumstances in which it was to be his lot to work in England. William of Normandy had married in 1062 the Countess Matilda of Flanders. But the two were related within the forbidden degrees. Since the pope could not prevent the marriage, he had excommunicated the disobedient couple and had laid the duke's lands under an interdict. William, whose love for his wife is the tenderest trait in a stern character and whose chastity is an especial honour in an unclean age, stubbornly refused to yield. Lanfranc, then prior in Le Bec, had been impelled by his legal instincts to utter a strong protest. The duke's anger flamed out against his opponent and included the convent in judgment. He insisted that the prior should be expelled, and gave orders that the convent homestead should be wrecked.

He even seems to have come down in person in order to make sure that his orders were carried out. At least the duke was in the neighbourhood when Lanfranc set out on his exile, so that the two met. For his journey the convent had provided their prior with a lame horse which could scarce carry itself. When the two men met, the exile bowed deeply to his superior, "the lame horse bowing his head too at every step." William took no heed of the salute; but Lanfranc cheerily bade him take heed of the ready obedience given to his command, and added that if the duke desired to be more speedily rid of his subject, it was necessary to provide a better horse for the journey. Something in the audacious humour of the petition, some shame perhaps at having been betrayed into anger with a monk on a lame horse, stirred the sardonic duke to sudden laughter. The ice was broken. Lanfranc had what he wished, the opportunity to state his position; and so dexterously did he state it that William ended by commissioning him to go to Rome and there patch up a peace with Pope Nicholas II. The artificial sin was atoned for by an unreal repentance. William and Matilda had their way, were acknowledged by Holy Church as man and wife, and bought off interdict and excommunication by founding, the one the monastery of St. Stephen, the other the nunnery of the Holy Trinity in the town of Caen. Thenceforward Lanfranc was William's right-hand man in all Church affairs, and was admitted so far as any man ever was to the counsels of that lonely spirit. The duke promoted his new adviser to be head of St. Stephen's in 1062, and in 1070 shortly

after his conquest of England sent for him to become Archbishop of Canterbury and Primate of all
England.

The two men had work enough to employ all
their energies in the new realm. The Church in
England had sunk in education, in discipline, in
spirituality. Already in Anglo-Saxon times it had
lost independence alike of government and of discipline. Church and State had become confused.
The prelates met in the Witenagemot along with
their fellow-dignitaries, the secular potentates. They
held also their separate councils at the same periods.
In a generation when the spiritual power in the
Church is strong and its spiritual aims are recognised such an arrangement may help to make men
see how the laws of a kingdom are something more
than a means for maintaining decent civil order, and
ought to be a means towards realising the kingdom of heaven on earth. But in a generation when
the Church grows weak in its special testimony, it
will only result in its deeper secularisation. Such
was the result then. And the fact that the separate
episcopal councils met alongside of the civil had only
brought it about that the decisions of the bishops
were regarded as having no validity, unless they
also received the royal sanction.

It is well, however, to remember that most accounts
we possess of the state of English religion in the
century are derived from men of the conquering race
or from men who were imbued with the new spirit of
the rising monasticism. A story is told of how Her-
fast, chaplain to the king and afterwards bishop of
Thetford, visited Le Bec and was presented by Lan-

franc with a child's alphabet as a study fit for his capacity. The incident may only illustrate the insolence to which culture gives sharper edge, and the prejudice which made the Norman incapable of seeing the sturdy qualities of Saxon piety. Yet when every allowance has been made, it would appear that the impulse of England's early conversion had spent itself and that the storms of conquest under Dane and Norman had brutalised the laity and lowered the tone of the clergy.

William, who hated all disorder, was ready to give his help that the house of the Church should be set in order, but the help must be on his own terms. He was himself a devout man. He was too keen-sighted not to measure the enormous power which the Church could exert to help or hinder the aims he cherished in his new possessions. But the Conqueror was above all a masterful man. Alongside of his own he could brook no other will. The more clearly he saw the influence which the Church could exert, the less inclined was he to suffer the control of this strong organisation to pass into other hands than his own. Of his own initiative he appointed and deposed bishops. Stigand, the archbishop of Canterbury, was set aside. Within a few years there was but one bishop who was not a Norman. They were not bad bishops, for as his conduct to Lanfranc showed William had an eye for a man. But they were all chosen practically by himself. The dying speech put by Orderic into the king's lips may have been uttered or not. It represents at least the impression which William's ecclesiastical action had produced on his contemporaries. " Never have

6

I dishonoured mother-Church: on the contrary it has
been the great desire of my life whenever occasion
offered to show her respect. Never have I made
traffic of ecclesiastical preferments; and as to simony
I have always detested and avoided it. In the choice
of dignitaries I have tried to find out sound doctrine
and meritorious life, and so far as in me lay I have
trusted the government of the Church to the worthiest
men that were to be had." The king's words about
simony were true. As Church dignities grew more
valuable the vice of purchasing preferment had crept
in, and crept in most where the Church's tone was
lowest. William hated it, partly because it offended
his religious sense, partly because he was too strong
a man not to despise that poor refuge of the men
who cannot make their way by ability. Save in one
instance there was never suspicion of simony in connection with any of the Conqueror's episcopal appointments. But there is a deeper simony than the gift
of money, and that is the surrender of a man's personal convictions. Now no man whose ideas clashed
with those of the king had any chance of rising to
prominence in the Church. Many of his appointments
were made from his court clergy, concerning whom
he had already sure knowledge that their course of
action would not run counter to his own.

It helped to maintain the dependence of the higher
clergy on the royal authority that so many of them
were Normans, alien in thought and sympathy to
their flocks. When Dom. Paul was appointed to
St. Alban's, Anselm wrote to commiserate him on
his banishment among barbarians, whose very language he could not speak. The gentle abbot bade

him remember how by life if not by word he could still witness for his Master, and urged him not to oppress his tenants by being greedy about his revenues. That an abbot in a foreign monastery counted it necessary to offer such advice is eloquent as to the relations which existed between Norman Churchman and Saxon flock. Relations of this character could only result in making the higher clergy a class apart who looked to the king for support.

It is fair to remember that the Conqueror was in a difficult position, and that his attitude towards the Church was not dictated merely by lust of power. He saw with the clearness of a man who had suffered from it the tendency of the feudal system to build up an oligarchy of narrow-minded but power-ful tyrants who considered nothing save the interests of their own order. The effort it had cost the duke to break down the barons' power in Normandy may have strengthened his resolution to do all in his power to prevent its equal development in England. There was no better counterweight than the higher clergy, whose brains and character could be cast into the scale against the gross bulk of the nobles. And at least it was the result, if it was not the purpose, of his policy that the clergy in England were driven to support, and to look for support from, the throne to which they owed their appoint-ment. The outcome of the policy can be seen in Anselm's later experiences.

As little as William in questions relating to the Church would suffer interference from within, so little would he brook control from without. "There-

fore he would not suffer any authority within his
realm to accept the Roman pontiff as Apostolic father
except at his bidding, or to receive his letters unless
they had first been shown to himself." Hildebrand,
shortly after he became pope, attempted to assert his
authority by sending a legate to England. Hubert
was commanded to remind the king of the services
the holy see at the instigation of Hildebrand had
rendered him by blessing the enterprise for the conquest of England. The legate was to demand a
return for the consecrated banner in the form of the
payment of arrears of the " Peter's pence " and an
oath of fealty to the pope. The answer was a curt,
dignified, but firm refusal. " Thy legate Hubert, holy
Father, came to me and warned me that I should
render an oath of fealty to thee and thy successors,
and that I should be more careful concerning the
money which my predecessors were wont to send
to the Roman Church. The one I allow, the other
I do not. I refused and do refuse to give the oath,
because I never promised it nor do I learn that my
predecessors have ever rendered it to yours. The
money, because I was busy for three years in France,
has been carelessly collected. But since I have now
by the Divine mercy returned to my kingdom, what
has been collected is being forwarded by the afore-
mentioned legate. The rest will be remitted as
opportunity offers by the messengers of Lanfranc our
faithful archbishop." When men on the Continent
heard that money was sent from the kingdom, they
said openly that England had become tributary to
Rome. William did not trouble himself about
the opinion of the Continent. He retained the

substance of his independence, and could let the shadow go.

Hildebrand baffled on this side sought to reach the king through the archbishop. He sent a somewhat imperious message summoning the latter to Rome. Lanfranc hesitated, but finally declined to come. The cautious terms in which the refusal is couched rouse the suspicion that William had read the letter and make it certain that the writer dared not go. And a clause or two in the pope's reply in which he rebukes his correspondent for over-subservience to the ruling powers prove that Hildebrand knew it. But the pope was shrewd enough to recognise that he could gain nothing in England except by force; and the position of affairs in Rome made it folly to venture on a quarrel with a ruler of William's quality. During the rest of the reign the Church in England was practically independent of Rome and free from all interference from abroad. Nor did the Church suffer much from its isolation. Only, since everything was made to depend on one man, there was no guarantee for the continuance of this better state of affairs. William, like many another strong-willed man, did not realise that he would not live for ever and that his passion for centralising all power in his own hands made it certain that confusion would break out after his death. There is a significant sentence in a letter from Lanfranc to Pope Alexander, before relations had broken off between the two courts: "I beseech you to pray God in His mercy that He grant a long life to my master the English king, for while he lives we have peace of some sort, but after his death we cannot hope to have peace or any other good." When the news of the

Conqueror's death did reach Canterbury, it caused so severe a shock to the archbishop that many thought he would die of fear and anxiety. Lanfranc's grief may have arisen in part from his knowledge of the character of Rufus, but in part it sprang from his recognition that all good order in England depended on the will of one imperious man who was mortal and who had been unwilling to recognise that an institution needs to outlive a man.

William's policy in thus isolating the Church in England has been described as disastrous. But during the king's lifetime it had little effect of a hurtful kind. There was a higher tone of religious life in France than in England. The stronger currents of a larger life bringing with them both good and evil were flowing there. Had they been all checked at the Channel, Britain would have lost more than it had gained. But the archbishop within the definite limits which were set to his activity worked hard to influence the religious life of his new country for good. To ignore other sides of his work, he bent his energies towards the reform of monasticism. William of Malmesbury relates that Lanfranc found the monks of Canterbury "not differing from seculars except that they showed themselves more reserved in chastity. For the rest they led a joyous life. One saw them go to the chase followed by hounds, lead horses, deliver themselves to amusement and good cheer. To judge by the number of their servants one had called them consuls rather than monks. At seeing these scandals Lanfranc for a time hid his grief. Not to terrify these lapsed monks by unsuitable severity he did not speak at first of reform. Only as opportunity arose he made paternal remonstrances and afterwards retrenched several abuses little by little." That the accusation is not more bitter is the better guarantee of its truth. The monks of Canterbury and of England seem to have been not evil or irreligious men but honest souls who were not over rigorous in the observance of their rule. They fulfilled their functions and consumed their revenues. But it is not difficult to understand how they must have been an offence to men of an austerer ideal, and especially to a man who had once found the Benedictine rule too easy and had contemplated retirement to a hermit's cell. These were not the stuff out of which a reform movement could arise, these men who were at ease in Zion, and whose honest spirits were unvexed by any high vision.

Since the archbishop found them the more difficult to reach with his new aims because every attempt at severer discipline was construed by them as a reproach on their past, he was driven to found new monasteries and to bring over monks from the Continent. Especially did he make liberal drafts from his old monastery at Le Bec. A bull was obtained from Pope Alexander, according to which the Archbishop of Canterbury must be always chosen from among the monks. There were now in Canterbury two convents. One, that of St. Augustine, was entrusted to Scotland, a monk from Mont St. Michel. The other was that of St. Saviour's, in which Lanfranc himself was abbot. Dom. Henry, who had made his profession in Le Bec shortly after Anselm, was brought over and made prior. So many monks passed between the two, that St. Saviour's became practically a succursale of Le Bec. Dom. Paul was appointed abbot of St. Alban's. Gondulf, Anselm's

closest friend, became bishop of Rochester, and there
built a cathedral and a convent with sixty monks.
Through the length and breadth of England the same
slow movement went on.

One weakness of Lanfranc's effort as of his mental
attitude was that heavy love for uniformity which
characterises all strongly centralised authority, and
which has made the Roman type so often blind to the
wholesome power which underlies freedom and indi-
vidualism. His inclination and that of the Norman
clergy generally was to despise the home effort and
piety. Once, when Anselm was in England on business connected with the convent, the archbishop consulted his visitor on a matter which was causing him
concern. The islanders persisted in offering reverence to various local saints whose names were not
recognised by the Roman authorities. To one in
particular his countrymen paid a peculiar veneration,
honouring his memory as that of a martyr. This man
Aelfeg had been Lanfranc's predecessor on the chair of
Canterbury, but in the judgment of his successor had
been martyred in no true sense of the word. The
Danes had taken him captive in one of their forays
and held him to ransom, with the threat of murder if
the ransom were unpaid. Their captive knew that
the only means of paying his ransom was to raise
the money from his poor tenants whom the Danish
invasions had already impoverished. Rather than torment them he had gone to his death. Could such a
deed be really called a martyrdom?

Anselm had no hesitation on the question. In words
which have a curiously modern ring about them he
declared his opinion that the man had died for the

right and to die for the right was to die for Christ.
Christ had once called Himself the truth and would
not disdain to accept the name of the right. Aelfeg's
might not be a death for the name of Christ: it was
better. It was a death for the reality of Christ.
Besides, were Lanfranc to urge his objection to its
logical end, he would need to strike off the list of
martyrs John the Baptist, who died for purity and for
truth, though Christ was never mentioned throughout
his whole trial. What difference is there between a
death for the right and a death for the truth? The
archbishop expressed himself convinced, conceived a
special veneration for his predecessor, and even ordered
Osbern, one of Anselm's pupils, to write the life of
Aelfeg and to have a passionale composed to his
memory.

In connection with this visit to England there is a
pretty sketch of the future archbishop's first appearance at Canterbury. His many friends had prepared
for him the reputation of a saint and scholar. He was
received with honour and asked to address the community of monks at St. Saviour's. The abbot delivered them a homily on how it is more blessed to
give than to receive. The quaint little address reeks
of the syllogism. Gravely and deliberately the speaker
proved how those who have just given him a dinner
have their generosity left after the dinner has dis-
appeared. Though his gratitude remained when the
table has been cleared, the kindness which produced
both dinner and gratitude was the greater. But the
convent gave him that day something more than a
dinner. Among the monks was one who listened
eagerly to every word which dropped from the abbot's

lips and whose heart went out in utter devotion to the
tender, strong man.  Eadmer became Anselm's devoted
admirer, to become in later years his confessor and
*baculus senectutis suæ* ("the staff of his old age"), to
become for all time his biographer.

The visits across the Channel grew comparatively
frequent, as the monks from Le Bec were scattered
throughout England, and as the possessions of the
convent increased there.  And wherever the abbot
went he won golden opinions.  Men in England loved
him, his geniality, his sympathy, his union of sweet-
ness and light, his power of being sufficiently at leisure
from his own thoughts to enter into theirs.  Men's
hearts among conquerors and conquered went out to
one who was neither Aostan nor Norman nor Saxon,
but a fellow-man among his fellow-men.  Even the
harsh Conqueror grew gentler in his presence.  "When
he sometimes came to the court of the king about
various items of business in connection with the
Church or with other matters, the king himself, laying
aside the fierceness which made him seem cruel and
terrible to many, became so kindly and affable that in
his presence he appeared, to the surprise of many, to
become a different man."

# CHAPTER VI

## ELECTION AS ARCHBISHOP

THE last years during which Anselm remained abbot at Le Bec saw two commanding figures disappear from the European stage.

In 1085 Gregory VII. passed to his rest at Salerno, murmuring as self-justification or confession, "I have loved justice and hated iniquity, and therefore I die in exile." There is no such tremendous figure in all history. A monk of humble origin he had risen to occupy the chair of St. Peter, and had risen through no arts of compromise or of flattery but through the unflinching advocacy of a few principles. He had lived first to dominate and then to divide into opposing camps all Europe, and he had done both by the appeal to an idea, the independence and spirituality of Christ's Church on earth. Alongside of Hildebrand, a man like Napoleon appears vulgar. It was to him an axiom that the Church was a divine institution, existing for specific ends and ruled by Christ's laws. Alike to manifest and to maintain its spiritual character, it must be freed from the control of everything alien to its own genius. The methods by which he pursued this single aim of his life and the conclusions he drew from this ultimate principle cost Europe appalling misery. No otherwise it may be than by such means could the heavy mass be leavened with higher thoughts. Canossa had revealed to astonished Europe the power of the Church when it appealed to an idea, but that power was too sudden to be enduring. And the exile into which the pope was driven, from which, himself a prisoner in the hands of his rescuers the Normans, he saw a nominee of the emperor seated on his chair at Rome, was the proof to all who cared to notice it that the struggle in which he had seemed victorious was only begun, and that many years would elapse before the opposing interests and ideals of emperor and pope could be brought to harmony. Into that struggle the abbot of Le Bec was soon to be drawn.

1087 saw the death of the conqueror of England in the priory of St. Gervais near Rouen. Suspecting his illness to be mortal, he had sent for Anselm. The abbot had hurried North but had fallen ill on the road, and lay sick in the priory of Sotteville across the Seine. The cathedral bell ringing to prime roused William from sleep, and caused him to ask what the sound meant. When his attendants told him it came from the Church of St. Mary, he lifted up his hands and praying, "To my Lady the Holy Mother I commend myself, and may She by her holy prayers reconcile me to her dearest Son, our Lord Jesus Christ," died.

What followed proved what he had been to his generation. Men told each other with awe that no sooner had the breath left the great king's body than his courtiers fled and left their master's body to be stripped by the scullions and deserted on the bare floor. No mere superstitious terror of the unhouseled corpse which death had surprised before the administration of the last rites of the Church drove men out in their pell-mell haste. They knew, and showed they knew, that the dam was down which had for many years kept back the forces of misrule in Normandy and England. Robert of Belesme, head of a great and unruly Norman house, was riding into Rouen to present himself at court. No sooner did the news of William's death reach him than he turned his horse's head. At Alençon and Belesme he made haste to expel the garrison of his dead lord, and to take joyous possession for himself. Men fled from the death-chamber to hold what was their own and to take if possible what belonged to their neighbour. The "Justicer" was dead; and, as everything had depended on his single arm, chaos threatened to come again. There could hardly have been a more eloquent tribute to the only strength which had been able to tame the baronage.

The body was brought for burial into the Minster of St. Stephen at Caen. The nobles were too busy with other tasks to attend, but the great ecclesiastics, abbots and bishops, were present. The Bishop of Evreux delivered an oration concerning the late king's life, and concluded it with an appeal to the assembled people to pray for the soul of the dead and forgive any wrong which he might have done them during his lifetime. "Then stood up Asceline son of Arthur, and with a loud voice in the hearing of them all put forward this complaint: 'The ground on which you stand was the site of my father's house which this man for whom you make request took by force from

my father, and utterly refusing justice he founded this
church by his strong hand. Therefore I publicly claim
this land, and in the name of God I forbid that the
body of the spoiler be covered with earth which is
mine, and be buried in my heritage.'" After due
investigation had proved the justice of the man's claim
they bought the ground in which the king was to be
laid. It was their fitting tribute to the memory of
him whose body they had assembled to lay in the
earth. When not blinded by passion or misled by
State considerations he had been capable of doing the
same. With many notable exceptions, with frequent
relapse into the lawless Norman temper, he had yet
recognised that there is an order in this world higher
than the will of the strongest. He too in his own
way had loved justice and hated iniquity.

On his deathbed William had bequeathed the
dukedom of Normandy to his eldest son Robert, and
expressed the wish that William, his second son, should
succeed him as King of England. And William II.,
knowing his England, had wasted no time in crossing
the Channel to take possession. To Lanfranc, who
crowned the new king at Westminster, he made
solemn promise of his purpose to rule according to
just and righteous laws. The nobles did not leave him
long in doubt that he would have to fight for his crown,
and were not long left in doubt as to his ability to
defend it. Many of them held lands on both sides of
the Channel, and foresaw the difficulty of an allegiance
which would now be due to two masters. Many would
have preferred the capricious Robert of Normandy to
his cunning and vigorous brother. Odo, the bishop of
Bayeux, whom the Conqueror in his last illness had

been persuaded against his better judgment to free
from the prison into which he had found it necessary
to cast his turbulent brother, gathered a strong force
and flung himself on England. But Rufus had the English people of Kent and the South, had also through his
father's policy and his own treatment of Lanfranc the
English Church behind him. By their help he struck
down the conspiracy for a time. But it was only for
a time. To the end he could never be sure of the
barons. They disturbed his reign by risings in the
North, and weakened his power by continual disloyalty.
It proves the shrewd statecraft, the indomitable will,
the unflinching courage of the man, that, though he so
soon quarrelled with the Church, he was able to maintain the unity of the kingdom against them. There
are many things to be laid to the charge of Rufus.
But, when the worst has been said against his private
character, his ecclesiastical policy, and his ravenous
ambition, one thing must be set in his favour that
the English people throughout his reign held fast to
him against the Norman nobles. Though he oppressed
them, his single oppression was not so dreadful as the
possibility of falling into an anarchy like that which
under the weak Robert soon afflicted Normandy. One
shearer was better than a dozen such. And England
was kept as England by his strong and brutal hands.

It was not long before the king's character began to
reveal itself in his public acts. He was a man of
coarse appetites, endowed with a hard clear intelligence, possessed by strong ambition, and alike ruthless
and resolute in carrying out his schemes. His father's
faithfulness to his wife is a tender trait in a grim
character; and it had been real enough to refine the

tone of his court.  The son recoiled into the grossest
debauchery.  Unmarried, he lived after a fashion which
startled an age that was not easily startled.  But his
debaucheries covered in him as in many another a
calculated selfishness which through all sensual indul-
gence never for a moment lost sight of the attainment
of its other and ultimate ends.  Of religion in any real
sense of the word the man seems to have been destitute.  That there was some power higher than his own
desires, which was capable of thwarting his wishes,
he did not question.  Therefore he hated it.  When he
submitted, he only submitted because he must and so
long as it was not safe to resist.  When he judged it
safe to resist, he did so without compunction and without remorse.  His repentance was terror, which existed
so long as he was in mortal fear but not for an hour
longer.  Freeman has well said that Rufus was what
this age never sees, a blasphemer.  To-day, if a man
wishes to live according to the desires of his own
heart, he either ignores all thought of the Almighty or
questions His existence.  Rufus could not find and did
not desire that easy way of escape.  He really believed
alike in God's existence and in His power.  And when
he found God in his way, he cursed Him in his heart.
To such a man the Church was an institution with the
fundamental ideas of which he was at hopeless variance.
It represented all that he most hated, it appealed to
that with which he had no sympathy.  It was useful
and could be made more useful in many ways.  It
could provide him with the instruments he needed,
men who had the best knowledge of finance and
administration which the time afforded, money which
his ambition and his pleasures continually required.

But as a means to discipline men's souls into obedience to the law of the living God he could only find it incessantly in his way.

There had sprung up in that period a type of Churchman of a peculiarly obnoxious description. In an age when almost all knowledge of finance, administration, and law was in the hands of men who had received a clerical training, and when the education necessary for such work could only be obtained through the Church, a number of men turned to that training as a means of securing secular preferment. They were often destitute of any higher insight into religion or of any interest in it for itself, but only in the monastic and episcopal schools could they obtain the knowledge which they desired for other ends. They accepted the outward forms of the Church in order to secure the power which its training was fit to give them. Thus they often added to their original vices the uglier one of hypocrisy and helped to dishonour the religion the outward symbols of which they bore. The Conqueror's centralised system of government which made a court chaplaincy the surest stepping-stone to ecclesiastical or civil promotion had attracted many such men.

From among these Rufus found the fitting instrument for his purposes in a certain Ranulf. He is said to have been the base-born son of a priest at Bayeux, but the strict party whose aim was to establish the celibacy of the clergy were branding as unchaste the innocent wives of many priests. Handsome, unscrupulous, clever, with the narrow astuteness of a self-seeking man, adroit to accommodate himself to the humours of those he served, this man rose from the position of a page to be Rufus' vizier. Someone about the court

nicknamed him Flambard, the firebrand, and the
name was found so adequate that it clung. The king's
passions and ambitions required money. Ranulf could
help him to gain it. He is accused of having falsified
measurements in the Domesday returns so as to
increase the ratable area; but the experience of
valuators in every generation makes one hesitate before accepting too readily the complaint of men whose
valuation has been raised. Certain it is that he used
every means to extort money from England. Henry
of Huntingdon is very emphatic: " With tributes and
exactions he not merely shaved, he flayed the English
people." Following the line of least resistance, he
turned naturally and inevitably to the spoliation of
the Church. Lanfranc was dead, and his death left
the Church in England without a head. Not only did
the rankest simony flourish in that every man who
was appointed to ecclesiastical office must pay for
the dignity received, but the king abused an old privilege. The sovereign was *advocatus* of all bishoprics and abbacies. During the vacancy of any one of
these he had the right to intromit with its revenues,
but could only employ the revenues for Church purposes. Rufus simply appropriated the larger part of
the income to the royal fisc. It became therefore to his
interest to continue the vacancy when any bishopric
fell vacant, and his father's policy which had made
all ecclesiastical preferment depend on the royal will
gave him the power so to do. After Lanfranc died,
the archbishopric was unoccupied for almost four
years. The king appointed officers of his own to the
management of vacant see or abbacy, assigned a certain
proportion of the revenues to the maintenance of the

clergy or monks, and rackrented the domains for his own benefit. The most immediate but not the worst result was a scandalous oppression of the Church tenants. Since the Crown did not hold the lands in perpetuity, its officers took little care of anything except the extortion of the largest possible sum during their occupation. But the worse and more abiding mischief was the destruction of discipline in the Church itself. The rising tide of religious life in England was checked.

All England groaned under the oppression. And what made the position of affairs more galling and more hopeless was that an appeal to the royal justice against the exactions of the exchequer became an idle formality. For Ranulf held the double office; he was, to use the phraseology of our own day, at once the Chancellor of the Exchequer and the Attorney-General. To appeal from the exchequer to the justice-court was to appeal from the firebrand to the fire. The laity must watch the gifts and lands which their fathers had left for the weal of their souls employed to maintain the royal pleasures or to subserve the royal ambition. To an age which was firmly convinced of the reality of Purgatory and the efficacy of masses to alleviate its pains that must have appeared a grievous wrong to the dead. But the mischief went deeper than Eadmer's vivid description of the conduct of the royal commissioners shows. Discipline within the Church was broken down. When several abbeys were headless, their revenues appropriated save for gifts doled out in niggardly fashion to the monks, no monastery could remain unhurt. When a bishopric remained vacant for years, the diocese fell into disorder. And when every abbey or see was filled only by a man who consented to pay for preferment, the tone of the whole Church was lowered directly and indirectly.   Several years of such rule would have sufficed to undo most of the efforts Lanfranc had made to introduce a higher ideal of cleri-cal life and Church government into England.   In the last year of the vacancy at Canterbury men in England were restless in temper; and many who had known Lanfranc had begun to say that there was no hope of a better state of affairs till Lanfranc's successor at Le Bec became his successor at Canterbury as well.

In 1092 Hugh the Wolf, Earl of Chester, fell ill. The by-name expressed a good deal of the character of the man.   A stout man of his hands, loving war and wassail, cruel and easily angered, he had followed William from Avranches to the conquest of England. The Conqueror having proved his fidelity and gauged his capacity had set him on the western borders to keep the wild Welsh in check.   Hugh knew his business and wrought his work in such rough wise as was revealed to him.   He fought well and lived hard.   But somewhere in his heart was a sense of unseen things which made the Church of Christ a reality to him, and with it went the rough respect of a man for vigour and sincerity, which made his admira-tion go out toward the men within the Church who were doing things.   Capable only of controlling other men, he could yet understand the higher dignity of men who could control themselves.   At Avranches the rough soldier had learned to respect the abbot of Le Bec and to admire the work of the Benedictines. Already in Chester, when he had wished to give some aid to religion, he had resolved to transform a house of secular canons in the church of St. Werburg into a community of monks. In pursuance of his scheme, he had invited Anselm to England, that the house might be reformed under his friend's direction and affiliated to the Norman abbey. Anselm refused to go. He could not pretend to be ignorant that men in England were thinking of him as worthy to fill the chair of Lanfranc. And while the matter was not before him in such fashion that he could either accept or refuse to undertake the duty, he was unwilling to expose himself to misunderstanding, as though he sought a dignity which he did not desire.

When he fell ill, however, Hugh longed for Anselm the more. In the day of his mortal need the man to whom religion was the supreme reality of life appeared to be the only man who could hear his confession and give his soul courage. When the abbot again refused to come, the earl sent a second and more urgent appeal. "Tell him that, if he comes not now, all the joys of his future bliss will not be able to make him forget that he once shirked his duty." The Wolf knew his man and knew how to lodge his appeal. Anselm still hesitated. But it was uncertain that the archbishopric would be offered him. What was certain was that a dying sinner needed him and craved for his presence. He resolved to fulfil the manifest duty, let the issue be what it might.

He had scarcely landed in England, when a message from his monks overtook him. Scarcity had again visited the convent, and there had been no Lanfranc to relieve their necessity. Probably the policy of Rufus in connection with ecclesiastical affairs had made the revenues from their property in the island kingdom

come in more slackly.   They charged their abbot on
his obedience not to return until he had put in order
the business of the convent across the Channel.   With
his double commission Anselm reached Canterbury,
where he had intended to celebrate the festival of the
birth of the Virgin.   There men hailed him as their
future archbishop ; and he fled.   On his way northward
he visited the court at Westminster.   Rufus showed
him high honour, left his seat and came down to receive him, brought him in and set him at his right
hand on the seat which Lanfranc had usually occupied.
The abbot asked for a private interview.   No sooner
were the two left alone together than he spoke to the
Red King about his scandalous life.   Gravely he set
before him the evil suspicions which were current
about his private morals and urged upon him the duty
of repentance and reformation.   The incident is significant.   To the monk the realities of death and judgment had so revealed themselves that his first business
was to recall a sinner from his evil way.   But the
worldly wise among the monks at Le Bec doubtless
shook their heads, if the story ever reached the convent.   They had cause to question whether their business was in the right hands, if they heard that their
abbot had used the opportunity of a private interview
not to make interest at court for his convent but to
attempt the conversion of the King of England.

Arrived at Chester, Anselm found the earl recovered
from his sickness.   The convent business detained its
head in England for nearly five months, but when that
was finished and the abbot applied for permission to
return to Normandy, the king refused to let him go.
It is too much out of keeping with all that is otherwise

known of William's character to believe that the interview at Westminster had made him desire to detain
the abbot in England or that he had any wish immediately to fill Lanfranc's vacant chair.   The more likely
cause was a political one.   Henry, the Conqueror's
youngest son, had lately secured a footing in Normandy.
A new count had succeeded in Flanders.   Robert of
Normandy was already showing his incompetence for
any sustained effort in government.   William had to
face the possibility of European complications, which,
as he always hoped to win something in Normandy,
might give an opportunity to his ambition.   But the
king knew the restlessness of nobles and people which
his treatment of the Church and especially the long
vacancy in Canterbury had caused ; he knew also
the common desire to see Anselm appointed to the
archbishopric.   He probably detained the abbot as a
useful pawn in his game.   What makes this supposition
the more likely is the king's consent to one of the
strangest contradictions which even the Middle Ages
can show.   At the Christmas court of this year in
Gloucester the bishops, abbots, and nobles of the realm
desired their king to allow prayers to be offered
in every church in England that God would put
it into their lord's heart to give an archbishop to
Canterbury and to his kingdom.   At first hearing of
the request Rufus was very angry, but he soon con-
soled himself by the consideration that, let the Church
pray as it liked, the final decision in the matter rested
with himself.   And he grimly suffered Anselm to prepare a form of prayer for the purpose, to which he
probably listened during the festival season.   It was
all part of the game.   If this would help to keep men

quiet, they might have their order of prayer as they desired. Their contentment enabled him to dip his hands more deeply and more easily into the revenues of the Church. The king's attitude of vulgar cynicism and his incapacity to appreciate the character of Anselm are equally marked in the reply he gave to one of his courtiers. The baron spoke highly of the abbot of Le Bec, as of one who had left all for Christ's sake and who in all his conduct sought for nothing less than the things of God. "Has he," sneered Rufus, "no eye for Canterbury?" "No," stoutly asserted the baron, "for that least of all." "Why," was the reply, "if he but imagined that he could get it, he would come leaping and clapping his hands at the chance. But, by the holy face of Lucca, no one shall be archbishop but myself." The character of Rufus, so far as his public acts reveal it, is one which gives subject for strange and difficult thoughts. He seems to have been almost destitute of the faculty to which spiritual things appeal. Nothing except material considerations appeared able to reach or influence him.

These now visited the king. In 1093 he fell dangerously ill at Gloucester. With his illness came such thought of religion as men of his stamp are capable of grasping. He was visited by mortal fear of death and judgment, and grew anxious to buy himself off from the God whose wrath he believed to rest upon him. Anselm who was near Gloucester at the time was consulted concerning the sinner's case. "Let him begin to the Lord with confession," was the abbot's advice. Thereupon Rufus emptied his conscience. He vowed reform in all his government. He promised to remit all charges due to the royal treasury, to open his

prisons and let the men he had oppressed go free, to
let fall every summons lodged in the courts against his
subjects. It witnesses to a strange state of English
justice, when these were regarded as of themselves
matters which required the king's repentance, and when
his first duty towards his God was to order all his pro-
cesses of law to be dropped. The descriptions which
Eadmer and others give of the oppression sound tame
before that witness. The king had all these pledges
written out and sealed with the royal seal. He promised a new rule of mansuetude and justice. And as
guarantee of his sincerity his rod of office was carried
to the church and laid on the altar.

But men asked one further pledge of their king's
sincerity. Let him name an archbishop for Canterbury. The appointment would be at once a public guarantee of his repentance and a check upon him, should he
desire to resile from it. There is something beautiful
in it. The archbishop was to those men still their
father in God; he stood for all that men desired to see
in England, an order which was not based on one man's
will but on the purpose of the Eternal. Rufus at last
named Anselm. The bishops went in search of the
new prelate that he might at once receive the staff of
office from the dying king. To their dismay Anselm
refused. It was no question of investiture or canonical
election which troubled him. He knew something of
his own power, but knew better than most men do
something of his own weakness. And the charge of a
great see, especially in the then conditions of English
religious life and under such a king as Rufus had
already proved himself, might well make a man of
his character hesitate. The bishops urged him to have

mercy on them and on England, lest his refusal should
harm the cause of religion. "I know, but I am old and
unfit for work. How can I bear the charge of all this
Church? I am a monk, and have shunned all worldly
business. Do not entangle me in that which I have
never loved and for which I am wholly unfit." The
bishops refused to listen. They promised to bear the
secular affairs for him—only let him become their head.
Finally they dragged him to the king's bedside. Rufus
from his sickbed added his entreaties. Let Anselm
remember the king's father and mother and their zeal
for Holy Church. Let him consider the estate of
the king's own soul, and show interest in his repentance by helping to make his reformation more sure.
But Anselm had ever great powers of resistance: he
still refused. The bishops fell on their knees before
him, he dropped to a like attitude and prayed to be
spared. At last they lost all patience. Archbishop he
must and should become, if not willingly then on com-
pulsion. A pastoral staff was brought and put into
Rufus' hand. But Anselm held his own rigidly closed
and refused to accept it. The men who surrounded
him strove to force his hand open. Some said they
succeeded in opening the index finger and closing it
round the staff. Others said the staff was held against
a closed fist. The men were in no mood to consider
trifles of that description, they were in that state of
nervous excitement when all sense of the decorous
disappears from their minds. This is naught which
you do, protested the struggling archbishop-elect. It
made no matter. They half carried, half dragged him
from the sick-chamber, brought him to the neighbouring church, and sang a hasty Te Deum over his election.

Anselm had good cause to write to his monks at Le Bec, " Those could not doubt my unwillingness, who on that day saw my face, as bishops, abbots, and other dignitaries dragged me protesting and struggling into the church, so that it seemed doubtful whether madmen dragged a sane man, or sane men a lunatic, save that they were singing, while I more like a dead man than a living grew pale with surprise and grief."

In the whole matter Anselm did not permit himself to be blinded by any illusions. The bishops, in the excitement of obtaining their desired object and in the hopes kindled by William's promises, cherished the expectation that everything would now go well. Not so their new primate : he was man of the world enough to know that a sickbed repentance is rather an insecure foundation, especially when the sick man is a Rufus. Brought back to the royal bedside he said to the king, " Know that you are not going to die of this illness. And be it also known to you this day that all you have done is nothing and can at any hour be undone." After the first excitement had grown quiet, he put his view of the situation before the bishops in a parable : " Know you what you have done this day ? You have yoked together in one plough a powerful steer and a feeble ewe. The plough is England's government, and the two who drag it are the king who rules over the temporal, the archbishop who governs the spiritual concerns. When both are strong, the plough drives on steadily. But you have harnessed me alongside of Rufus, and the untamed indomitable steer will break loose again and drag, not the plough only, but his fellow in the yoke through briars and across the wilderness. You will gain no profit from this or from me."

And in truth they form a strong contrast, the Norman full of the pride of life and almost untouched by thought of the things which though unseen are eternal, the Goth to whom this life was but a preparation for that which was to come and who could only grow interested in any aim so far as it represented an eternal truth. It was hopeless from the beginning that they should ever understand each other, more hopeless that they should long succeed in working together. A more adroit man, a second Lanfranc might have managed the Red King. But Anselm was little able to see any common ground between two opposing principles: he was equally incapable of betraying one which he held. When once his stand was taken, the consequences which arose as a result disturbed him very little. He could only remain in the position to which he was committed, vexed and astonished because his opponents failed to appreciate his attitude. The very passionlessness of his adherence to conviction helped to deceive men like Rufus who fail to understand that a man who does not bluster and never dreams of intriguing can yet be in deadly earnest over any question. Having almost no personal rancour, cherishing no small jealousies, the primate was ever ready to be reconciled to an opponent: not understanding his opponent's attitude, he was helpless to bring about the reconciliation he passionately desired. He could not form a party. The party might form itself round him or round the convictions which he represented. Decidedly no weak ewe this, for beneath the meek exterior there lay hid a more tireless and indomitable resolution than under the bluster of the king.

The election and the delivery of the pastoral staff

from the king's hand were alike irregular.   Of formal choice by a duly-constituted ecclesiastical court there is no mention.   Practically Anselm was chosen by acclamation in a body which could regard itself as uttering the voice of England.   The court gathered beside the king's bed was Norman England; its voice was the voice of Norman England.   When the king nominated the new archbishop, he became the mouthpiece of their selection.   Even if there had existed a court which was competent to nominate a successor to Lanfranc, it could not have met without the king's consent, and Rufus refused to allow freedom to these courts.   As little could the delivery of the pastoral staff by the king be called regular, when the deed is judged by the standards of a later age.   It is possible to insist that Anselm by opposing a closely clenched fist to the staff declined to receive it from the royal hand.   But that the staff came from Rufus was not the ground of his refusal.   He declined it from any hand.   His unfitness for the duties which the office imposed, the peculiar difficulty of fulfilling its duties under a king like Rufus, his unwillingness to leave a cloistered life were the reasons which according to his own express declarations prompted the refusal.   Had the other question presented any difficulty, he was not the man to have been silent about it.   Despite the protests of Père Ragey and Mr. M. Rule it remains clear that " we do not find Anselm expressing the slightest scruple as to receiving the archbishopric by the gift of the king only without reference to the elective rights of any ecclesiastical body."   It may make the archbishop a neater lay-figure wearing the label "investiture question" to think of him as provided with a series of ready-made decisions on the problems of Church government and as then proceeding to put them into practice. But it is more in agreement with the facts of the case to recognise that he became a strong supporter of the new canons of Church law because he found that not otherwise could he attain the ends which he saw to be essential to the prosperity of the Church in England. Nothing which the archbishop wrote at this time (and he wrote much especially to his monks at Le Bec) betrays the slightest hint that the question of the method of election had then occurred to him. The reason was simple: his mind was wholly occupied with the prior question as to whether he could accept the office on any terms.

And that was the question which vexed the leading minds of England for some weeks. The new prelate raised difficulty after difficulty. He was unfitted by nature and training for the management of secular affairs: his bishops promised to relieve him of these. He urged his vow of obedience as abbot in Le Bec: they undertook to convince his monks. He fell back on his allegiance to his archbishop in France and to Robert of Normandy: they would persuade both to free him. And then they opened the whole battery of duty. He knew the state of religion in England and how much depended on whether the see of Canterbury were worthily filled. Dare he suffer it to fall back into the king's hands? If he judged himself incapable of the task, had he any right to set his private judgment against the judgment of all England which had solemnly asked him to undertake it? After many struggles Anselm consented, and the letters were written to Normandy to announce his decision and to request his superiors to set him free from his duties there.

But the man now found himself in a difficult position. His decision was sure to expose him to misunderstanding, and much of it was the direct result of his past action. He had spoken strongly—perhaps the new circumstances brought the suspicion that he had spoken too strongly—about the necessity of a cloistered life. Many had been persuaded through writings or words of his to flee the dangers of life in the world and to seek refuge at Le Bec. When he the head of the convent elected to return to the world's turmoil, there was no one but himself to blame, if some of the monks who had sought the monastery at his persuasion turned his own words against him. The first letter to Le Bec breathes that feeling throughout, and the frequency with which he returns to the point betrays the consciousness that the reproach is not unjustifiable. And he could do nothing except fall back on his own clear sense of right and appeal to their knowledge of the general course of his life before this time. "I hear that there are some (but who they are God knoweth) who in malice feign, or through error suspect, or by intemperate grief are driven to declare that I am rather attracted to the archbishopric by evil greed than compelled by religious conviction. And how can I persuade these of my good conscience in this matter, if my life and conversation satisfy them not? For I have so lived in the monastic habit during thirty-three years (three years without office, fifteen years as prior, fifteen as abbot) that all good men who knew me loved me, not that my zeal brought this about but the grace of God: nor did any man see in me any deed on which he could base the conclusion that I delighted in advancement. What then shall I do? How shall I repel this false and hateful suspicion, that it may not by diminishing their love hurt the souls of those who for God's sake loved me, or by persuading them that I am worse than I am (hurt the souls) of those who are misled by evil example or admonition, or even by setting before them a bad example the souls of those others who knew me not and may hear of this." And he went on to call God to witness that only duty had compelled this step, and to pray God to correct him if the step proved to have been a wrong one.

While the letters were being sent to their destination in Normandy, the king recovered from his sickness. His repentance endured no longer than the sickness. When his health was restored, he became ashamed of his remorse and sought to wipe out the memory of it by new severities. Orders were issued that all prisoners who had not yet been released should be more closely confined than before, and that as many as possible of the released should be recovered and shut up again. The suits against his subjects which had been dropped were continued with greater rigour. The short breathing-space of hope made the later condition seem but the more intolerable, so that the monkish historian wrote that "such misery arose in the realm that all men who remember it remember it as unique in England." When the Bishop of Rochester ventured to remonstrate, the king replied with a scoff, "You may as well understand that by the holy face at Lucca God will never make me good as a result of the evil He has done me."

When the letters which set the abbot free to under-

take his new duties arrived from Normandy, Anselm
sought the king at Rochester.   There he laid before
William the three conditions on which he was prepared to accept the archbishopric.   The king must
restore to Canterbury without process of law all the
lands which had belonged to the see during Lanfranc's
tenancy, and must consent to have the question of
the lands which even Lanfranc had not been able to
secure brought before the courts for decision.   He
must further understand that in the division between
pope and antipope Anselm with all Normandy had
already acknowledged Urban II. to be the legitimate
successor of St. Peter, and that from this allegiance he
did not mean to resile.   And finally the king must
promise due respect to the archbishop's counsel, even
as the archbishop owned the king to be his liege lord.
There was a party at that time in the kingdom which
combined with strong convictions as to the independence of the Church in England high views on the royal
prerogative.   Their work has largely passed into
oblivion because their effort failed, but enough remains
to prove that they were by no means contemptible
in ability.   Had Rufus been less of a pagan, had he
not made the royal prerogative a mere means of extortion in ecclesiastical affairs, he might have been
able to maintain his father's position to the Church
in England.   At this time he was guided by the advice
of this party.   He laid Anselm's proposals before
William, bishop of Durham, and Robert, Count of
Meulan, and by their counsel replied that everything
which Canterbury had possessed in the days of Lanfranc would be handed over to the new archbishop,
but that about the other property of the see he declined

8

to give any pledge. As to the question between the
rival popes, since Anselm had asked for no understanding, William proffered him no promise. In a short
time, however, the letters from Le Bec and the
Norman court reached the king also, and he seems to
have thought that Anselm was now completely in
his power. No longer abbot in Normandy, not yet
archbishop in England, the man was in the king's
hands. Acting perhaps on the advice of Flambard,
William decided that he had promised too much, and
at Windsor requested as a personal favour that those
parts of Lanfranc's lands which had been granted out
on military tenure should be continued to the men
who held them. To this Anselm refused to consent.
To grant away any part of the property of the see
even before he was consecrated was practically to make
himself guilty of simony.

Matters seemed to have reached a deadlock. Already
Anselm began to hope that he might escape from the
whole charge and without any neglect of duty might
be free to become a simple monk again. But the
position irked the nobles. Their religious sense was
hurt by seeing the primacy of England used cynically
and publicly as a means of huckstering for money.
And even men who had little sense of religion had reason
to dread this bold stretch of the royal prerogative and
to fear that the king would not limit himself to such
treatment of religious property but extend his claims
to secular also. The moment was propitious for their
voice being heard, since the king was contemplating a
descent on Normandy and could not afford to alienate
their support. Rufus yielded. At Winchester on
April 17 Anselm put his hands within those of the

king, and " became his man." Thereupon he was duly
seized of all the temporal possessions of the see of
Canterbury even as Lanfranc had held them. At
Canterbury on September 25 he was enthroned; and
finally at Canterbury on December 4 1093 the Archbishop of York with nine assisting bishops consecrated him to the primacy over all England. It was
the custom of the age to practise a species of *sortes
Biblianæ* on the occasion of the consecration of a
priest. A book of the Gospels was opened over the
shoulders of the kneeling priest. The passage at
which the book fell open was held to possess some
prophetic significance. Men whispered to one another
that the passage which was read over the bowed head
of their new archbishop was that which relates how
a certain man made a great feast and bade many, but
they all with one consent began to make excuse.

# CHAPTER VII

## ROCKINGHAM

A CUSTOM had existed from early times in England, according to which a bishop on receiving his appointment paid heriot to the king like any other who had succeeded to a fief. And, although since the middle of the tenth century this had ceased to be compulsory because in that form it savoured too much of simony, it still continued in the form of a voluntary gift. Accordingly, when Anselm appeared at Yuletide in the king's court, he brought with him a present of 500 pounds of silver. Rufus, who was busy fitting out an expedition against his brother in Normandy, was even more in need of money than usual. The gift was welcome, but some of the courtiers whispered that it was insufficient. Canterbury was wealthy, and the archbishop who owed his promotion to the royal bounty ought to acknowledge his debt more worthily. Anselm was informed that nothing less than 1000 pounds would satisfy the king. He refused to give it. The lands and property of the see had been so robbed by the officers of the exchequer during the vacancy that only after three years had elapsed was its new occupant able to live without forestalling his annual revenues. The money could only have been procured by oppression of the tenants. Besides, the archbishop's whole instincts revolted against the idea of buying his liege lord's confidence as one buys an ass. "Do not, my lord," he urged, "refuse to accept what I now offer. For though it is his first, it will not be your archbishop's last gift. And I judge it to be more useful and more honourable to thee to accept from me a little with loving goodwill and often rather than by violent exaction to extort much at one time and against my will. With goodwill thou canst have me and all mine at thy service, but compulsorily thou shalt have neither me nor mine." Rufus brusquely retorted, "Let thine own remain thine with a curse to it, mine own will suffice for me; and begone." There remained nothing for the archbishop to do except to comfort himself with the reflection that the refusal had freed him from even the appearance of having bought his see, and to distribute the silver among the poor as alms "for the good of the king's soul."

In February 1094 Rufus gathered at Hastings an army for the invasion of Normandy, and thither the bishops of England also gathered to bless his departure and pray for his success. Since adverse winds detained the expedition for a month, the opportunity was employed to consecrate one of the king's chaplains, Robert of Blouet, to the see of Lincoln. The archbishop sought to make a further use of the opportunity. It was near the beginning of Lent. The camp was swarming with young gallants whose flowing hair and effeminate style of dress gave colour to the suspicion that they were addicted to certain vices. The archbishop delivered a vigorous

Ash Wednesday homily and persuaded many to abandon at least their long hair. But his spirit was ill at ease. To him had been committed the care of the moral and spiritual estate of the realm. He believed that, unless something were done, the kingdom threatened to sink into practical heathenism cloaked by the Christian name, yet without the royal support he could do very little. A more practical man would have recognised that the eve of a warlike expedition was not the time to press Church reform on the attention of Rufus, but Anselm was resolute to make the attempt. Admitted to the royal presence, he went straight to the root of the matter. There was no discipline in English religion, there was no means by which the archbishop could make his influence felt on the whole land or by which the Church could utter its voice. If only king and archbishop united their forces, they were able to effect something for the support of tottering Christianity within their England. What, Rufus asked, did the archbishop desire? Let the king appoint men to the vacant abbacies, so that the monks might no longer be at liberty to transgress all rule and live as they listed in their monasteries. And let the Church be free to exercise its ancient right of holding synods. During the king's lifetime none had met in England. If the king suffered one to meet now, and if the canons it enacted were supported by the king's authority, something could then be effected to prevent the land from becoming a very Sodom. "And what will all this do for you?" sneered Rufus. "For me nothing in all likelihood, but much for God's honour and for yours." The king blustered that the abbeys were his property,

and that he meant to maintain his hold on them as
tightly as the archbishop maintained his hold on the
lands of his see. "To you they belong," was the
answer, "but to you as their guardian, not as their
owner; they are yours to employ for God's end not
for your own ends, to rear men for God's service and
not warriors for your battles." The place where the
archbishop uttered the words might have proved to
him how ill-timed they were. Rufus was in instant
need of troops and money to pay them, and was
least likely then to surrender an easy source of
revenue.

Anselm was unwilling to give up the effort to reconcile himself with the king. Except they twain could
plough a straight furrow, there could be no harvest in
England to the good of the Church of Christ. At his
request the bishops went back to the court to ask why
he did not have his lord's grace. "I see no special
reason why it should be given," was the dubious answer
to their petition. The primate was unable or unwilling
to construe it, but his bishops helped him out. "Give
him money, and he will then see the special reason.
Give him much money. We have all required to
do it, and you need not expect that you alone can
escape." But this Anselm utterly refused to do.
Apart from all other considerations, if he were to yield
now, what guarantee had he against further and larger
demands? At least, the others urged, he could give
the original 500 pounds which he had previously offered.
No, he refused to give even that. He would not consent
to offer a gift which had been already rejected. And
if he had been willing to give the sum, he could
no longer do so, for the money was already in the

hands of the poor to whom he had caused it to be distributed. "Tell him," was William's reply, when this
answer was reported to him, "that I hated him yester-
day, and I hate him more thoroughly to-day. Let him
be sure my hate will grow with the following days. I
will never again count him father and archbishop.
I hate and refuse alike his blessing and his prayers.
Let him begone whither he will." There was nothing
more to be hoped. Anselm could but leave the camp
and retire to Canterbury, while William unfurthered
by his archbishop's prayers crossed into Normandy.
And there, Eadmer adds, meaning no doubt that it was
the inevitable result of the want of those prayers, he
gat for himself no profit proportioned to the money he
spent, but came home baffled. The money spent in
Normandy was not however wasted, for Rufus could
bide his time.

The incident is significant, and rightly seen it shows
what the struggle for the liberties of the Church
meant in those days. The archbishop after election
received his temporal possessions at the hands of the
king by the symbolic gift of a pastoral staff, paid homage to his sovereign, and was then consecrated to office
by the Church. It seems a trifle to invert that order
and claim that each bishop must be duly consecrated
to his pastoral duties by the Church, and only then
receive his temporal possessions from the king. But
the order of procedure showed what in the view of the
Crown was the relative importance of the primate's
functions. In the royal view the see of Canterbury was
a fief held of the Crown, conferred by the Crown, bur-
dened like all others with certain duties to the Crown.
Unlike the other fiefs, it involved certain spiritual

duties and required certain spiritual powers in its possessor. These powers the Church conferred on the man to whom the Crown had already given the fief, and these duties the primate must fulfil to the Church. But the scene at Hastings proved how Rufus understood the order of procedure. The State's claim came first. The duties which the archbishopric like any other fief in England owed to the Crown, duties of providing soldiers and supplying money, were in his view paramount. And when his ambition dictated a war in Normandy, he meant, even at the risk of dislocating and impoverishing all the religious activities of England, to use the bishoprics and abbeys as a means to his end. The other duties could and must wait until these temporal necessities were satisfied.

Anselm may have chosen an inopportune time to urge the needs of the Church. That was the mistake, if it was a mistake, of a man of absolute singleness of purpose to whom the first duty of the Church was to care for the morals and the religion of England. Was every effort for the spiritual good of the kingdom to wait on the royal will, on the chances of peace and war, on whether Rufus needed the revenues of abbeys and sees to prosecute his own schemes? It was no mere academic question as to the order of procedure which Churchmen fought for, when they claimed that the consecration must come first, and that Church not king should have the right of investiture. The order was merely the outward symbol of the inward reality, that the spiritual duties of bishop or abbot ought to have precedence. The question was a most practical and urgent one, as it revealed itself on the beach at Hastings. Anselm was fairly involved in

it, and was never during the rest of his life to be
free from it.   It was inevitable, as matters then stood
in the Church, that he should sooner or later turn to
Rome.   For the Roman see had shown under Hildebrand that it understood the gravity of and the wide
issues involved in the question.

At this period the Roman see had recovered from its
temporary defeat in Hildebrand's exile and death.
Urban II. who succeeded the feeble Victor had won the
upper hand in Italy.    Matilda the great Countess
had practically conquered Henry IV.; his wife and
son had betrayed the hapless emperor into the hands
of the papal party.   Clement the antipope still held
part of the city of Rome, but his power was so
negligible that Urban could venture on leaving Italy.
In the following year the pope would at the Synods
of Piacenza and Clermont launch the first Crusade,
and win new support through the deed.   The respect
which Urban won as representative of a purpose
which was uniting all Christendom lent an increased
moral weight to all his other edicts, and the pope
was shrewdly calculating on the fact.   The Crusades
seem far enough away from the investiture debate.
Directly and indirectly they helped to determine its
issue.

Since the time of Augustine's landing in England it
had been considered essential to the exercise of his
episcopal functions that each archbishop within a
year of his consecration visited Rome and received his
pallium at the hands of the pope.   The pallium itself
had become a stole of white wool in which four black
crosses were inserted to represent the four cardinal
virtues.   Woven from the wool of two lambs which

were annually consecrated on the festival of St. Agnes at her church without the walls of Rome, laid on the tomb of St. Peter on the night preceding the festival of the apostle, and blessed at his altar on the day of the festival, the stole was meant to symbolise the purity which ought to characterise its recipient within and the obedience to the holy see which ought to distinguish his conduct without. The benediction which was pronounced over it as it lay on St. Peter's altar closed with the prayer, "May this be to him a symbol of unity and a mark of perfect communion with the seat of the Apostle." That it must be claimed within a year of consecration was one of the significant rules by which the Church declared that none of its dignitaries was fully qualified for his office until he had received recognition from the Church itself. It was an act which might in one age fall into a formality and in another rise to the dignity of a principle, but the maintenance of which gave the Church its opportunity. In the days of its weakness the Church could suffer the full significance of the deed to fall into the background; in the days of its strength it could insist on all the meaning of the rite and use its unquestioned existence as a means of assault.

William had already during the year showed his jealousy of any interference from Rome. When Herbert Losange, bishop of Thetford, repented his simony in paying 1000 marks for his bishopric and went to Rome to entreat pardon from the pope, the king summarily deposed him. It was therefore to be anticipated that he would raise difficulties over the question of the pallium. In November the war in Normandy was over, and troubles along the Welsh marches brought the king back in haste. In December 1094 or January 1095 Anselm visited him sore from his failure at Gillingham near Shaftesbury and asked leave to go to Rome for the pallium. It was already more than a year since the archbishop's consecration, and he could therefore now receive it only by the special grace of the pope. The king asked to which pope he meant to go. "To Urban," was the reply. "But," answered the king, "I have not acknowledged Urban. And, according to the practice of this realm both in my father's time and in my own no subject within the kingdom can acknowledge a pope without the king's leave. To challenge this right is to attempt nothing less than to take from me my crown." It was in vain that the archbishop reminded him how he had before accepting consecration given fair intimation that he did not mean to desert the allegiance which along with all Normandy he had pledged to Urban. The man, who shortly after his own consecration told one who reproached him for not remaining true to his word that it was impossible for any man to keep all his promises, was not likely to be very sympathetic with such a scruple. He reiterated that no one could acknowledge Urban without disloyalty to the service due to the king. The general question was then and still remains deserving of full consideration. Anselm however refused to accept its determination on the mere dictum of William. He asked that the question should be referred to a great council of the realm. At the same time he frankly warned the king that, even if the decision went against him, he dared not break his oath to Urban, and must in that event ask permission to leave the kingdom until the king's decision for that pope enabled him to return with a clear conscience. This frankness with which Anselm always treated his opponents confused them as much as it helped him. They did not understand a man who imported sincerity into diplomacy. William and his advisers seem to have been unable to understand that when the archbishop gave his word he meant to keep it, and to have believed that either the allurements of office or the fear of the royal wrath must be sufficient to move him in time from his pledged word. And the only reward they received for their distrust in their adversary's honour was that they went to the decision of a great constitutional question with their hands tied. It must certainly be counted to Rufus for moderation that, instead of following his father's example and deciding the matter by his own will, he summoned a council at all. But by having permitted the archbishop's consecration with full knowledge of the pledge to Urban, by allowing himself to believe that threats could move Anselm from a clear pledge, he surrendered half the strength of his position in the eyes of all fair-minded men in England, and prejudiced the general question by uniting with it the individual case of the archbishop.

On February 25 1095 a great council of lords temporal and spiritual was held at the castle of Rockingham. The castle, which the Conqueror had built " quite as much for the purpose of coercing the inhabitants as for the protection of the glowing furnaces," lay on the northern edge of Northamptonshire, and was probably chosen for its present purpose because of its being a central place to which all England could come for so important a cause. The sittings were

opened on Sunday in the church of the castle. The
king himself was not present, but kept himself apart
with a few of his special counsellors, of whom the
chief were Robert of Meulan and William of St.
Carileph, bishop of Durham. The former was an
astute Norman, strong and clear of purpose, skilled
in all the intricacies of feudal law, and with an intellect sharpened by the hundred points of casuistry to
which it gave rise. The latter was a clever intriguer,
ambitious, with more volubility than brains and more
audacity than either. He has suffered the bitter fate
of the loser in a great question, when the history of
the struggle is written only by the winners, and has
been represented as a mere court-bishop who hoped to
flatter the king and by truckling to his wishes win
for himself the archbishopric which he helped to force
Anselm to renounce. But the two men at this time
represented a policy of the hopelessness of which the
Bishop of Durham later convinced himself. They
stood on other grounds than mere self-interest for the
divine authority of State and king in England. An
expression used by John of Salisbury sums up the
attitude of Robert of Meulan, "The true majesty is
only that of God. The crime of *lèse majesté* can only
be called such because the king is on earth the representative of God." It was no base ideal, the one which
our Northern forefathers had in their minds when they
refused their kings a poorer descent than that from
the gods. And it would have been well for Europe
had the Church recognised the truth which it contained.
Churchmen could then have been fairer to their opponents, and they might have prevented men from
thinking of patriotism and justice as mere natural

virtues, and from thrusting aside the affairs of the State as purely secular concerns.

In the nave of the castle-church the bishops and nobles were met, and messages passed and repassed between them and the king's privy council. Anselm stated the position with grave simplicity, making no appeal to religious passion but speaking as he might have done to a class of his students at Le Bec. "The king had declared that, since he had not acknowledged Urban, he would not allow the primate to seek the pallium from that pope. And if Anselm received Urban or another as pope without the royal authority, or if having already acknowledged him he held to his determination, he was by that deed acting against the faith which was due to the king." Was this the law of England? That was the matter which they must decide. But the archbishop went on to add somewhat to the bishops about the position in which he found himself. They all knew how he came to be their primate, and that the office was none of his own seeking. They must recognise his declaration that but for his fear of contravening the will of God he would rather have been cast into the fire than accept the office. They had persuaded him to put aside his own wishes and to undertake the burden, and they had promised their help in connection with the secular affairs in which he recognised his incapacity. The time had now come when he had a right to look for their guidance and help. Let them give him both, and remember the seriousness of the question they had to face. "For it is a serious matter to contemn and deny the vicar of St. Peter; it is a serious matter to deny the faith which according to God I have pledged to the king: but this is no less serious, which has been said, that I cannot hold fast the one without denying the other."

The council was in a grievous dilemma. The man before them had given his allegiance to Urban. In an hour of grave danger, to save themselves and the Church in England from a difficulty, they had called on him to undertake his present office. He had accepted it, but had taken care to define the terms on which alone he consented to undertake it. They had slurred over his conditions in the hope that something would turn up, that things would arrange themselves, that their pledge would not need to be redeemed. And now their promise was being claimed to the full.

The answer which they gave was exactly what might have been expected from men who had been elected to their office as these were. The Conqueror had expelled simony, but he had sold the Church to pliability. As the bishops had bent their necks to enter, they were the more ready to bend their necks to remain. The superior clergy were not wanting in knowledge or piety; but they were Normans, aliens in sympathy and in tongue to their flocks, thrown as we have seen into dependence on the court. They abounded in expressions of confidence in the wisdom of their archbishop. He was so little in need of advice from his suffragans, that he had rather wisdom enough to advise both them and himself. But, if he still insisted on knowing their mind, they offered him the same counsel which in like case they would follow for themselves. Let him submit himself absolutely to the king's will, and surrender Urban. The king would acknowledge a pope, when it pleased him. The archbishop would join with him in that recognition, and then everything would again go well. No doubt there was the possibility of the king not acknowledging the right pope and of Anselm as a result being in a worse position than before. But men in a difficult situation have a fine power of closing their eyes to the unpleasant possibilities of a course of action which promises to deliver them from a present difficulty.

A great deal of unnecessary contempt has been poured on the bishops. Certainly theirs was not a heroic policy, and, what often counts more in the judgment of men, it was not the one which finally triumphed. But it is necessary to realise the situation which lay before them. They shared in principle with all Churchmen of their day the as yet undefined idea of the supremacy of the chair of St. Peter. But men had grown accustomed to regard the papal authority as not conferred by the Church, but as capable of being exercised only by one who received his appointment through the emperor. The Empire had not lost its sacrosanct character in men's minds. The popes were seeking to bring another idea before men, but they did not succeed till many years after this date. Still in men's eyes it was the business of the temporal power to acknowledge the pope. In England all intercourse with the papal see had been interrupted during several years without great direct loss to the state of English religion. What his bishops recommended Anselm to do was to continue the policy which had been followed by Lanfranc under William the Conqueror. The men believed, and, until time and the character of Rufus proved its impossibility, had a right to believe that that policy could be maintained. To men who hold the papal supremacy to be

9

of the substance of the faith their attitude must naturally appear to be a treachery to principle. But it is ever the misfortune of studying history in the light of a later dogma that it makes the student incapable of appreciating the motives of the men who were still fighting out the dogma, and that it converts all Church history into a series of black and white figures which is hopelessly unlike the real Church-life men see around them every day.

On the Monday the council met again. Anselm renewed his question, to receive the same answer. Now the matter which the bishops' answer overlooked was that the archbishop had already given his allegiance to Urban. Perhaps the night had given some of them opportunity to realise that they the religious leaders of the people were advising their primate to go back on his plighted word. At least some appeared to be ashamed and hung their heads. There was silence for a short time. At last Anselm gathered himself together and rising from his seat while his eyes flashed in his excitement he spoke. "Since you who are the shepherds of this Christian people and you who are named leaders of the nation deny counsel to me your head, save according to one man's will, I go to the Chief Shepherd, the Angel of great counsel. I take from Him the counsel which I follow in this which is not merely my cause but His, and that of His Church. He has said to the most blessed of the apostles, 'Thou art Peter and on this rock will I build My Church.' Again He has said to all the apostles, 'He that hears you hears Me, and he that despises you despises Me, and whosoever touches you touches the apple of Mine eye.' It was first to St. Peter and in him to the other apostles, it is first to the vicar of St. Peter and through him to the other bishops that these words as we believe were spoken,—to no emperor, king, duke, or count. But that in which we must submit to earthly rulers, the same Angel of great counsel teaches, 'Render to Cæsar the things that are Cæsar's and to God the things that are God's.' These are the words and the counsels of God. These I accept, and from these I decline to depart. Know therefore that in the things of God I will render obedience to the vicar of St. Peter and that in those which pertain to the earthly honour of the king my master I will render him true counsel and ministry unto the best of my knowledge and power."

The bold declaration irritated the assembly. They angrily refused to become the bearers of such a message to the king. Anselm unwontedly stirred went into the inner room and delivered his message in person; then leaving the king angry among his troubled counsellors, he came back to his place and quietly fell asleep. There was a long delay. The king's party had evidently come to the council without a clear plan of action. They had misunderstood the man with whom they had to deal, had mistaken his gentleness of nature for flaccidity, and had hoped that when he found himself alone against the whole court he would surrender his position. They had no further advice to offer except a repetition of the old method. In the late afternoon accordingly the king's messengers returned to the church and bade the archbishop understand that this must come to an end. He had troubled the kingdom long enough and roused the indignation of all its chiefs by his presumptuous attack on the royal prerogative. And this

prerogative of the Crown which he had assaulted was
that which their king valued most, since by virtue of
it he was superior to every other king in Christendom.
William declined tamely to submit to its surrender,
since even if he were willing his people would be
wounded in their pride by his submission.  And as for
Urban what after all could he do for the benefit of
the archbishop?  To win Urban's approval would
bring him little good, if in the effort to win it he
embittered his king against him.  And if by surrendering the point he could win the king's favour,
what harm could Urban's anger do to him?  Let him
assert his freedom, let him be free as became an archbishop of Canterbury from any foreign interference,
and when he had surrendered this point everything
would go well.

The cynicism of the argument wearied the archbishop, already jaded by the unwonted excitement of
the day.  A man of his high nature is not unwounded,
when religious men speak as though a promise were
nothing, and as though self-interest must outweigh a
man's loyalty to his word.  And to one who saw how
much England was in need of a moral reformation and
who found that the men who ought to have helped him
to effect it were prepared to advise their archbishop to
weigh his loyalty in the scales of profit and loss it
must have been a heavy blow.  He told them wearily
that he was not prepared to abjure his pledge to Urban,
but that, if they allowed him a night's rest, he would
answer them to-morrow as God guided him to speak.
Perhaps he distrusted his own power of self-control.

But William of St. Carileph had promised the king
either the resignation of the archbishop or his renuncia-

tion of the pope. And now he misunderstood the man. Surely Anselm was wavering. Surely the loneliness in which he found himself had shaken his nerve. If they pressed him home now, they must certainly win. He came back from the king with a message couched in bullying terms. There was to be no delay, unless he was prepared to yield the point. " Without that the king adjures the hate of Almighty God on himself, and we his lieges unite in the adjuration, if he allow an hour longer this delay for which you ask till to-morrow."

It was the last bolt, and with a weaker man it might have succeeded. Except for Gondulf of Rochester, Anselm found himself forsaken by the episcopate. He did not know the temper of the nobles, and had no right to expect them to move in his defence, when his clerical brethren failed him. A stranger unable even to speak the language of the people to whom it was his lot to minister, alone in the darkening church, he deserved to be forgiven had he surrendered. But his answer was as decisive as it was quiet. " Whoever would prove that because I will not renounce the obedience of the venerable bishop of the Holy Roman Church, I violate my faith and oath to my earthly king, let him come forward, and he shall find me ready to answer him as I ought and where I ought." The check was met by countercheck. And the counter-check was a defiance which made the bishops pause. Whether they in the heat of their eagerness had forgotten the fact, or had counted on the monk's ignorance of the immunities of his see, is uncertain. But Anselm had hit the weakness of their position. They could not even try him. The only court which was

competent to do so was the court of Rome. The
baffled messengers could only retire.

And in the gathering dusk where the frail monk
sat wearied among his few supporters a sense of the
dignity of this one man who alone in all England dared
to show front to the dreaded Rufus crept into the
minds of some among the commons. Suddenly a knight
detached himself from the rest, and kneeling before
the archbishop bade him be of good cheer. " Remember how holy Job on the dungheap routed the
devil and avenged Adam whom the devil had routed
in Paradise." The quaint, uncouth words went round
the archbishop's heart like wine. For it is something,
let a man have fought for as high ends as he will and
be fully convinced of the righteousness of his cause, to
know that he is not alone. Probably the knight knew
little about the immediate issue of the struggle, understood little about papal claims and royal rights. But
the English sense of fairplay was appealed to, and that
deeper sense of the right to appeal to law against the
tyranny of power which has rarely deserted the race.
It was a day to be marked with a white stone in the
cause of English liberty and English law, the day
when the lustful arrogant Norman kings learned
that there was a limit set to their power, and that
any man, monk, priest, or layman, dared resist their
will.

What the knight showed that the English commons
had seen the Norman nobles were to learn next day,
that Anselm was fighting a battle which involved the
rights of every man in England. Among the royal
counsellors there was great dismay. They knew not
what to advise. They could not gainsay Anselm's

position, for they agreed with him in his interpretation
of Scripture: they did but follow the usual practice of
disliking its application. There was no desire on their
part to abjure the pope. But now Rufus began to turn
against them. The king felt that he had been led into
a position where defeat was sure to lessen his authority
more than if the whole question had never been raised.
Naturally, being the man he was, the Red King began
to show his teeth in an unpleasant way to the men
whose advice had helped to bring him into his present
difficulty.

When the morning of Tuesday came, William of St.
Carileph had no better counsel to offer than violence.
The king was free to take what the king had given, ring
and pastoral staff. Let him in the exercise of his royal
prerogative depose the presumptuous prelate who had
dared oppose him. The plan suited the clerical party
in the council, since by means of it they threw the odium
of removing Anselm on the king. But the laymen
interfered. Had there been any fault in the archbishop, they might not have done so. England was not
then so satisfied of the inviolability of the clergy that
they would have risen to prevent a king from unfrock-
ing a discreditable prelate. But the archbishop was
not merely a great ecclesiastic, he was also one of the
chief nobles of the land, who like themselves held a fief
at the king's hand. If one of their class untried and
uncondemned could be stripped of title and property by
a mere act of the royal will, which of them all could be
accounted secure? They too came to see that, because
of the way in which William had elected to regard the
matter, the archbishop stood for the question whether
common justice any longer endured in England. And

they like the commons closed round him, if only for
their own sake.

But what was now to be done? Something must
be done forthwith, for the king swore that he was prepared to brook none as his equal in England, and that,
if his counsellors did not show themselves willing to
wreak his vengeance on Anselm, he meant to wreak
it on them. Grimly Robert of Meulan described the
situation. He spoke with the keen enjoyment of a
man who loves the finesses of law for their own sake,
and who cannot help admiring the dexterity of an
opponent, even when that dexterity threatens to spoil
his own favourite schemes. " Truly I know not what
to say. We arrange the long day through a scheme.
We talk it over and determine how it is going to hold
together. And meantime he sleeps and troubles himself not. But no sooner has the scheme been laid
before him than with a breath of his lips he bursts it
as if it were a cobweb."

At last the king himself hit on a strange scheme.
Though the bishops as Anselm's suffragans could not
try him, they could at least deny him their obedience
and their brotherly fellowship: the king for his part
did hereby deny him all furtherance within the realm.
The unhappy bishops had gone too far to retreat.
There was nothing to be done except to proceed on the
way they had chosen. So they went to their archbishop and bade him understand he need no longer
expect fellowship or obedience from them. Anselm
gravely replied that for his part he did not find it quite
so easy to renounce duties which he had once vowed to
fulfil. As he had taken his solemn vow of all Christian
service to the king, the see, and England, he meant,

while he remained primate, to maintain his vow and to fulfil his duty. Their renunciation made it more difficult adequately to fulfil the duty; but difficulty absolved no man from duty and least of all from a duty which he had pledged himself before God and Holy Church to fulfil. And this answer he begged them to bear to the king.

It was the simple answer of a Christian gentleman, but it dissatisfied and embarrassed the Red King. He had hoped to drive the harassed primate to resign. He turned to the nobles who stood by, and asked from them the same renunciation of their obedience. The nobles however declined. "We were never his men, nor can we abjure an oath of fealty which we never swore. But this he is—he is our archbishop. It is his to oversee Christian religion in this land, and we who are Christian men cannot reject his oversight, while we are in this land, and especially while no stain of wrong which can justify your action is found in him." The laymen of England had proved themselves more quick to the appeal of honour, more ready to see the claim of justice than its Churchmen. The single fact is sufficient proof of the need for reform within the Church in England.

But the bishops must drink the cup of their degradation to the dregs, for again the king demanded from them what precisely their renunciation of the primate implied. Was it unconditional, or did they only renounce obedience to him, so far as he spoke in the name and by the authority of the pope? According to their answer was the treatment which was meted out to them. Those who renounced Anselm without any reservation were retained in favour, but those who admitted any reservations in their abjuration required to show reason why the king should continue favourable to them: the cause was shown after the fashion they had once recommended to Anselm, by liberal gifts of money.

The archbishop resolved to quit the kingdom. Whether he proposed to go to Rome for his pallium, or whether he had cause to fear that Rufus' denunciation of protection left even his personal safety insecure, he demanded a safe-conduct to the nearest port. But this did not suit the king's plans. He dared not suffer Anselm to go beyond sea, practically a banished man, and the living proof of his king's injustice. For the primate of all England to fall into his brother's hands in Normandy would be for Robert to win a strong support. And, although Rufus had been once defeated in the duchy, he had not the least intention of surrendering all hopes of a final conquest. Besides, the attitude of the nobles and commons had startled the royal counsellors. A truce was accordingly patched up between king and archbishop. Until the next Whitsuntide the question should remain undetermined, and meantime nothing should be done by either party to prejudice the question or to molest each other. Rufus observed the truce as might have been expected of him. While Anselm lived quietly on the manors belonging to his see and strove by every poor means left to him to strengthen discipline and raise the standard of morals in the Church in England, the king worried him in paltry and evil ways. Baldwin, the archbishop's right hand, to whom we suspect it was in no small measure due that Anselm was able to steer cautiously through the many difficulties in which he had been involved, was banished. And the royal officers tormented the unhappy dependants of Canterbury with unjust and ruinous charges until the poor wretches complained it had been better for them in the days when they had no archbishop than it was under their present head. Something however had been won. That Anselm had been able to withstand the Red King's anger, to defy his utmost power and yet to go free in England was in itself a promise of better days for English liberty. And it was further the educator of a sense of justice in the hearts of Englishmen, without which the new liberty would have been worse than useless, and without which a casual victory on a question of Church politics must have remained trifling and ineffective.

# CHAPTER VIII

## THE RUPTURE AT WINCHESTER

THE primate was now very solitary in England. His encounter with the king had shown how little community of spirit existed between himself and his bishops. Gondulf, his friend of the cloister, was near at Rochester, but Gondulf could follow, he could not advise; he had made of Anselm in the years at Le Bec the whetstone on which he sharpened the edge of his piety and principles, he did so still. The lonely and harassed man turned longingly to the monastic life from which he had been dragged to govern the Church in England. Among the monks at St. Saviour's he felt himself at home. He had once called Le Bec his nest, he now half playfully, half wistfully spoke of himself as an owl: "When I sit here among my fledglings I am at peace. When I am among those secular affairs, I am like an owl in the daylight, which flies helplessly amid attacking daws and crows." But then the fact that he could not conscientiously remain at St. Saviour's, that he had accepted tasks which he could not fulfil, smote him; and he fell to weeping among his monks. "Have pity upon me, O my friends, have pity upon me, for the hand of God has touched me." He was primate of all England,

140

responsible in his measure for the condition of religion
there; and the Church's work was not being done in
England. A less sensitive spirit might have thrown
the entire responsibility for that on the conditions
which hindered him. But the man who had once
written concerning the simpler decisions of the individual conscience, *Terret me vita mea* ("My life appals
me"), was capable of a keener self-reproach, when he
realised the far-reaching influence upon other lives
alike of his action and his inaction.

What was within his power he still wrought. At
the request of Murierdarch, King of Ireland, two monks
were instructed and consecrated at Canterbury for
the bishoprics of Dublin and Waterford. In later
years he continued to watch over and guide the king
and his new bishops. There are numerous letters to
abbeys and religious houses in England, which can
date from this period alone. But a new tone appears
in the archbishop's letters. Out of them has died the
happy spontaneity which through the lumbering school-
Latin lends a charm to the letters from Le Bec. The
English letters are more professional. They are no
longer written by a man to whom the kingdom of God
is the supreme interest in life to another about whom
the writer can take it for granted that the same is
true. They are not written in the happy confidence
that the reader judging their spirit will not be quick
to condemn an unguarded expression. The writer
knows that every sentence will be weighed. The
letters remain a source of information on the condition
of ecclesiastical affairs: they more seldom give a
glimpse into the life of a man who trembles before the
judgment and the mercy of his God. Responsibility

and factious opposition have touched this pure spirit with their harsher influences.

In some directions the archbishop was difficult to educate. It was a period when men in hours of mortal sickness or peril were willing to vow to the Church gifts which they afterwards heartily grudged to pay. Men gave a farm to Holy Church, and then sought to litigate the bishop out of its rent. The conflict lent a zest like that of battle to the piping times of peace. And the fact that king and archbishop were known to be in opposition gave men courage to encroach upon the rights of the Church. Anselm was ill fitted by nature for scuffles of that description. When he was forced to interfere in the struggles which human passions provoke, disgust overpowered him and he became positively ill. "What would you?" he said. "I have for so long a period banished all love and all desire for the things of this world, that I can find for them neither force nor zeal. I confess it: when these melancholy interests come to assail me, it is to me a horrible apparition, and I shudder as a child does at the sight of some hideous object." His advisers told him that his tenants were swindling him, that many were advancing claims which they themselves knew to be unjust. "What?" he answered. "Are they not then Christian men? Do they not make their assertion of the truth and righteousness of their cause without flinching? It cannot be that they thus perjure their own souls for the sake of a little gain."

An impracticable dreamer some of the warriors and busy Churchmen of the court doubtless judged their primate to be. Yet he was a man who in the few things about which he greatly cared had a will of

steel. His very indifference about the other matters
made him more impossible to move. That too they had
begun to discover and were to discover more thoroughly
in later years. And the strangeness of the discovery
in the life of their leading Churchman stirred in the
more thoughtful a curious wonder whether Christianity
does not after all mean to seek first the kingdom of
God and His righteousness.

The large simplicities for which and among which
the man lived told on the consciences of men. They
could not but be stirred by the witness among them
of one who behind the pomp of the archbishopric
maintained the austerity of the monk (almost more,
Eadmer hints, than befitted a great prelate), and who
bore it not as a yoke but as a gracious habit which
had ceased to be felt a burden. What monasticism at
its purest has always represented was preached among
them by the life of their chief bishop. Those who
were admitted to the archiepiscopal palace were
astonished by the plainness of its dress and food.
When the reader at the dinner-table entered on a
subject which interested the archbishop or read a
passage in Scripture which seemed to demand explanation, Anselm was wont to use it as the theme of a
discussion. And men noted that when he talked he
ate most, for then one of his fond monks made it his
business to supply his master's plate with food, which
he ate more abundantly, because he forgot what he
was doing. In the private meals of his household
he appeared to live on a mere trifle. Yet did he
urge those who finding him wait for them hurried
over their meat to be nowise embarrassed on his
account. And, did he see one who relished his food, he

looked at him smilingly, and lifting his hand gave
his benediction, " May it profit the eater." These are
trivialities, but they impressed a man who was
Anselm's companion and who was also an Englishman.
The fact that he counted them worth mention in the
Life of the archbishop suggests that self-control in the
common appetites had become strange in the eyes of
Englishmen, and that there was a wonder to them in a
life which even in trifles practised the grace of self-
denial.

Anselm however was and felt himself wearily alone.
The matters which interested him most, the questions
of theology and metaphysics over which he had
brooded at Le Bec, were of a nature for which no
man cared in England. The matters which he had
been appointed to regulate were withheld from his
interference. And meantime England seemed in
morals and in faith to go from bad to worse. No
synod could be held without the king's permission.
No decision of the archbishop had any force without
the king's support. For all such matters Rufus cared
nothing at all. He had his own aims, which he pursued
with a high courage and a resolute ambition. But it
rested on Anselm as a continual burden that to his
care was delivered the charge of Christian religion in
the realm. There was little he could do save live a
holy and a simple life. But was that all which the
Church in England and its Head had a right to expect
at the hands of the primate ?

Suddenly a royal edict appeared which announced
that Urban was recognised as pope in the kingdom.
There had been a special reason why the king was
unwilling to suffer Anselm to leave England while still

seized of the archbishopric. With the cunning which often passes for statecraft he had during the negotiations at Rockingham secretly despatched to Rome two of his chaplains, Gerard and William of Warelwast. They were instructed to make inquiry as to the state of affairs between the rival popes and by acknowledging one secure from him the pallium. At that time Rufus was still hopeful that Anselm could be persuaded to resign or compelled to demit his office. With the pallium in his own hands the king designed to institute a new archbishop and invest him with the coveted stole. By this means the royal prerogative would be materially advanced, since the king thus secured an apparent right to confer not merely ring and staff but even the pallium. That part of the scheme was shattered by the firmness of Anselm and the barons. But if the king had suffered the archbishop to go beyond sea still invested with his dignity he would have been left with the useless pallium in his hands.

William however had to deal with subtler brains than his own when he met the leaders of the Roman Curia. His envoys finding Urban in possession of Rome acknowledged him on behalf of their master. But the pope entrusted the precious sign of office not to them, but to Walter, cardinal bishop of Albano, whom he appointed legate and sent to England in order to investigate the whole position of affairs. The mission itself was a gain for Rome — no legate had been allowed to enter England since the early years of the Conqueror. The first anxiety of the legate was to make sure of the king and of England. Accordingly he had no sooner landed than he hurried through Canterbury without halting to confer with the primate, and made his way to the court. Men were astonished that Anselm who had suffered for Rome was ignored in this fashion, and were still more astonished when they saw the yielding attitude which Walter adopted toward the king. They began to whisper that Rufus had gold at his command and that the Curia was ever venal. But the legate played his cards with great dexterity. By flattery and apparent submission he persuaded the king to issue the decree, which acknowledged Urban as pope in England. But when Rufus demanded that the legate should by virtue of his authority depose the troublesome primate, the scene was changed. Now nothing was heard of except the extreme gravity of deposing an archbishop without any form of trial, and the reminder of how, whatever Anselm had been as a subject of England, he had committed no wrong as metropolitan. As to the pallium the legate refused to deliver it up, and urged delay in order that a reconciliation might be effected. It was no part of Rome's policy to suffer the stole to be conferred by lay hands. Rufus tried the means which he believed to be omnipotent, a large bribe to the cardinal and to the papal court; but this was absolutely declined. Justice was now inflexible. The king found he had committed himself irrevocably to Urban, and had nothing for his pains.

All that remained to be done was to make the best of an evil bargain, and to use the pallium as a means of extorting money from Anselm. By this time the truce agreed on at Rockingham was nearly at an end. The archbishop was summoned to meet the king at Windsor. He came to one of his manors near Hayes and was there met by a number of the bishops who asked whether he was prepared to make peace by the payment of a sum of money to the king. Anselm had grown weary of the sordid business. More bluntly than usual he refused; he declined to reveal to the world that the friendship of his sovereign was put up for sale. Probably the bishops thought that the fact needed no revelation at that time of day, for they merely asked what was his alternative. Anselm answered that he had seen no reason to alter his former resolution and wished to repeat his request for a safe-conduct out of the kingdom. The bishops then informed him that he need not leave England, for the pallium was at Windsor and could there be obtained from the legate. Surely in these circumstances he would pay for this sign of honour, and give at least as much as his journey to Rome with its inevitable heavy expenses would have cost. "Honour," sighed the weary primate. "God who reads my heart knows in what esteem I count an honour of that nature." But he was resolute; pay he would not.

Rufus was beaten at every point, and he knew it. Other cares of state however claimed his attention. The king had trysted to the Whitsuntide court a very different guest from his gentle archbishop. Robert of Mowbray, Earl of Northumberland, had failed to appear at the Easter court in Winchester. The Dark Earl had always been suspect. He had been concerned in the conspiracy which almost ousted Rufus before he had well become king. Since the king had long desired revenge and had recently had cause to suspect fresh conspiracy in the North, he had issued an ultimatum requiring his subject to appear at Windsor, or abide the issue. Mowbray, with some other of the

Northern barons, had failed to appear. William, who never threatened unless he meant to fulfil, was mustering his strength for war. The attempt to extort money from Anselm had doubtless been prompted by the necessities of the war. When this hope failed Rufus fairly threw up the game. He received the archbishop and showed a more friendly spirit than at any time since his consecration. While the two sat together in presence of the assembled court, the legate entered and after the fashion of legates abounded in seemly platitudes. Behold, he said, how good and joyful a thing it is for brethren to dwell together in unity. He had not, Eadmer adds drily, done anything to promote that unity. However, after the fashion of his kind he sat down and talked about it.

A slight difficulty threatened at the last moment to disturb the peace. In order to save the king's face, Anselm was asked to accept the pallium from William's hands. But the archbishop had learned what important conclusions could be read into the simplest forms. He had fought for the stole as a dignity which the king was incompetent to confer : to receive it now at the king's hands was merely to surrender the principle which he had asserted. It was accordingly arranged that the legate should lay the precious treasure on the altar at Canterbury, and that thence Anselm should take it as a gift from the Church itself. Legate Walter arrived at the city 27th May 1095, and was met at the gates by a long procession of monks who came out to do reverence to the symbol of papal authority. The procession was closed by the episcopate of all England, between whose ranks walked their primate clad in the full robes of his office but bare-

footed. The pallium was borne in and laid on the
altar. Anselm kneeling lifted it, kissed it, presented
it to be kissed by the bystanders, put it on his shoulders,
and now at length acknowledged by king and pope as
Primate of all England and Archbishop of Canterbury,
proceeded to celebrate high mass in his own cathedral.
Behind him the reader read the Gospel for the day.
And again as had happened at a like ceremonial he
read that a certain man made a great feast and bade
many, but they all with one consent began to make
excuse. All who heard noted the coincidence, and
some may have realised how the final power of all
ceremonies whether of royal or papal institution rests
on the faith of the multitude in their value.

There followed for Anselm a year of outward peace.
William was too busy with the Northern troubles to
seek new methods of worrying his archbishop. He
showed an unwonted clemency toward the Church
and even an alacrity in filling some of the vacant sees.
Baldwin and the other monks who had been banished
during the truce were permitted to return. Herbert of
Thetford had his bishopric restored. Within a year
after the death of the Bishops of Worcester and
Hereford, the king filled up the vacancies, the former
by the appointment of Samson of Bayeux, the latter by
that of chaplain or clerk Gerard. Both were consecrated by Anselm in St. Paul's in London, June 15 1096.

Whether the change in the king's temper made men
think it prudent to show themselves friendly to
their archbishop, or some of the bishops began to be
ashamed of their past conduct, two of the episcopate—
Osmund of Salisbury and Robert of Hereford—had
followed Anselm on his way to receive the pallium at

Canterbury and craved forgiveness. It was no sooner asked than given. The primate did not even wait till they had reached the city, but leading the way into a little church by the wayside absolved them there. Others were inclined to submit, but were unable to repent frankly. They strove to justify their past action, and they found support, where it might least have been expected, from the papal legate. That dignitary had not yet quitted England; he remained to complete the work for which he had been sent. Anselm in the eyes of Rome's legate was worthy of support, but was not sufficiently ultramontane. He had fought against Rufus for the property of the Church and for the due recognition of Urban, but he had accepted ring and staff from the king. The archbishop must be brought into closer sympathy with the new claims of Rome. Walter set himself to trouble the scrupulous spirit of Anselm.

When William marched North, he summoned the archbishop to Nottingham to bless his arms, and entrusted him with viceregal powers over the south and east of England. The king's enemies on the Continent were not unlikely to seize the opportunity of his absence in Northumberland, in order to attack Kent. In the exercise of these new duties, Anselm was confined to Canterbury: to leave it would have thrown him open to the suspicion of neglecting duty. To him with this fresh anxiety the legate wrote requiring him to attend an interview, at which they might confer about the appalling abuses under which religion was suffering in the realm. The sudden request from one who had studiously ignored his position seems to have nettled the gentle saint. It was impossible, he wrote, for him to leave his post even for that important end. Besides, if they did meet, any decisions at which they arrived were worthless without the consent of the king: an interview therefore in Rufus' absence was wasted time. But Anselm further suggested that the legate who now professed so deep an interest in these questions had already had many opportunities for the interview he craved during the days he spent at court and kept himself carefully aloof from the archbishop.

In his reply Walter showed his aim more clearly. One cause of the religious condition he found in the unhappy relations between the primate and his suffragans. The latter were troubled but were not prepared to take on themselves the entire blame for the situation. They had found themselves unable to support Anselm, because he had done homage to a schismatic king, *i.e.* to one who had not accepted Urban as pope, and had submitted to consecration from bishops who for a like reason were in schism. Anselm fairly roused tore the flimsy excuse to tatters. " Certainly I knew not then, nor do I now know that they have been in schism, and, to use their own word, separated from the Church. . . . In reality they did not reject the authority of the pontiff, as little did they deny that Urban was pontiff: they were but uncertain because of recent troubles and therefore postponed their recognition of him. No judgment had ever cut them off from the Church, they confessed themselves submissive to the Holy See ; it was under this profession of obedience that they consecrated me. Further our lord the pope knew that I had been consecrated and by whom, and to which king I had offered homage; yet he sent me by the mean of your charity the pallium usually given to the Archbishop of Canterbury, not as to a schismatic but a recognised bishop. By that he has confirmed my consecration. He who has been the instrument of this confirmation, my lord Walter, bishop of Albano and cardinal, knew all these things when he fulfilled the commands of the pope. If this accusation seemed serious to you, why did you not speak to me of it before conferring the pallium? If it seems to you contemptible, you yourself can judge how you ought now to spurn it under foot. You call God to witness that so far as lay in your power you have defended my cause, and that this has prevented you until now from completing your mission. I thank you for your goodwill to defend me, but am not aware that on my side you have met any hindrance in the completion of your mission. Your Reverence says that you have been unable to confer with me and with the others as much as you have wished. It is for you to know the cause of that inability. For myself I know that I long and strongly wished to speak with you before I had the opportunity: even when I was able, it was a more scant opportunity than I had desired."

The saint could hit hard when he chose. A man who owned that power of restrained and courteous irony and used it so rarely exercised a self-control of which few men who wield the pen are capable. And there are some to whom such self-restraint will appeal more powerfully than the fact that he slept hard and ate and drank like a hermit.

The legate left England. To all appearance he had

not much to show as the result of his mission, but in reality he had done his work. He had secured England's recognition of Pope Urban, and given nothing in return. He had dropped anxieties into the mind of Anselm which would bring him nearer Rome. Mabillon has suggested that the whole aim of Walter was to extract money from the archbishop in return for the pallium. That may be the case, though the suspicion rests on nothing higher than the most venomous type of gossip, the gossip of the cloister. The man was carrying out in his own way the policy of Rome, and as events proved successfully. Lanfranc had practically lived beyond the control of Rome, and had governed the Church in England without its interference, though in theory he had never thought of denying papal authority. We have seen how the established practice gave rise to theory, and how men who found independence practicable began to ask whether it were not as well to cast off even the forms of allegiance. How far the archbishop shared this spirit Rome did not and could not know. The legate was there to find out the state of affairs, and had a free hand to work toward rebinding this *papa alterius orbis*—this pope of a second world—to the central authority.

The method he took was cruel but effective. He wrought through the scrupulous conscience of the primate. Anselm was able to disprove all his charges; but they were sure to rankle. There *were* irregularities in his election. He had paid homage to Rufus, and the papal court was forbidding homage with a new stringency. It was true that Urban had sent him the pallium and so recognised him, but those things remained. The legate's hint about his inability to do all he wished for the correction of abuses could be repelled, and the condition of affairs shown to be due to no negligence on Anselm's part. But the hint rendered more acute the primate's sense of impotence and need for outside help. The legate of the very court for whose prerogative he had fought passed him by and left him to learn the object of the mission from a royal decree. That might have been a piece of insolent discourtesy on the part of a cardinal, but it might have been an official act. This man was the pope's legate. Was not his view the one which would be represented and might be accepted at Rome? Did Rome count his election dubious, his position uncertain, his loyalty unreliable? These things which a man whose position was happy could lightly and easily have tossed aside sank into and rankled in the lonely and troubled heart. He must go himself to Rome. Already in a letter in which he sent to Urban his thanks and a gift for the pallium he found it necessary to excuse himself for not coming to Rome on the ground of the troubled state of Europe, of his own precarious health, of the difficulty of his relations with the king. An event which soon followed precipitated the desire into action.

For a period the affairs of the Church had not busied Rufus. His energies were needed for other tasks. He flung himself fiercely against De Mowbray in Northumberland. When the conspirators shut themselves up in Bamborough and thought that its stout walls must exhaust the energies of the assailants, their king built a tower to shut them in. The Welsh had risen at the news of the revolt and were harrying across their borders. His tower made Rufus able without raising the siege of Bamborough to march against the West. The terror of his presence was sufficient and the invaders withdrew within their own frontier. The king satisfied himself with some random harrying which increased their terror, and hurried back to capture the obstinate fortress and wreak his long desired vengeance on the rebels.

This took place during 1095. In November of the same year Urban held the great council at Clermont, and by his fiery eloquence kindled the first Crusade. Directly that movement left England untouched, the enthusiasm seemed to be quenched in the Channel. Neither the king nor the archbishop, though for very different reasons, ever showed much interest in its progress. But indirectly it influenced the politics of the kingdom and the fate of Anselm. The Crusade sprang into vigorous life in Normandy. Among the many who took the cross was Robert, its count. His versatile mind, easily captivated by an outward form of devotion which had little moral claim, found food for what it called its religion in the excitement. His vanity was appealed to by the prospect of heading the movement. He resolved to go, and, since his dominions must not be left unguarded and ungoverned, since his empty purse must be replenished, he determined to secure the one and fill the other by pledging the county of Normandy to his brother of England. It was William's opportunity of gaining without a blow the foothold across the Channel which had never ceased to be the secret object of his ambition. A bargain was struck, according to which William agreed to pay his brother 10,000 marks and to hold Normandy in pledge during three years. The money could be wrung from England; and as for the restitution, even if Robert ever returned, he might return in no condition to demand the restoration of his rights.

William never had any money, he had to wring the marks from reluctant England. Since the sum was in a remote sense required for furthering the ends of the Church, there was more apparent right than usual in extorting part of it from the Church. To raise the required sum, relics were sold, missals and gospels were stripped of their costly coverings, gold and jewels were torn from altars. Anselm thought himself bound to offer his share. He needed to borrow the 200 marks from the conventual chapter at Canterbury, but in return pledged the revenues of his manor of Peckham to the monks for seven years.

In 1096 William crossed into Normandy to take over the administration of his newly acquired property. But the restless Welsh broke into England, so soon as his strong hand was lifted from them. He hurried back in February 1097 and repelled their attack. When that was done, the king had reached the summit of his ambition. At peace within his own realm, he was the master of Normandy. One thing was needed in order to satisfy him, that he should succeed in breaking the one man who had dared resist his will and so be free to despoil the Church of its possessions. The opportunity was found in the contingent which the archbishop had furnished for the Welsh war. Anselm was summoned to answer

in the king's court for having sent to his king's
need a body of ill-found and ill-trained troops. Most
writers on the period take it for granted that the
complaint was unjustified. More probably it was
well based. Anselm's high qualities as a Churchman
make it but the more likely that the charge was
true. Himself incapable of overseeing the equipment
of men-at-arms, he was the very man to be cheated
grossly by those to whom he entrusted the task.
The complaint with all it implied is but another
illustration of the confusion into which Church
and State had slipped. So long as Churchmen
remained an integral part of the feudal system,
holding high office as liegemen of the king, owing
the military and secular service which their office
implied, the claim of the Church to choose its own
dignitaries and in that choice to consider nothing
except their spiritual qualifications was bound, if
yielded absolutely, to weaken the State. The better
Churchman a bishop was, the better saint and scholar,
the better fitted to fulfil what the Church required
from him, the less likely was he to be capable of fulfilling that side of his functions according to which
he must be ready to aid his liege lord, in peace by
counsel, in war by armed help. It is well to recognise
that in this quarrel the whole right did not lie
on the side of the Church. So long as Churchmen
clung to the dignities in virtue of which they enjoyed the privilege of high position with the inevitable condition of being required to fulfil certain
civil functions, so long the State which had regard
to its own self-preservation could not allow the
question of fitness to fulfil those functions to be

ignored in the election of the men who held the dignity.

One thing however was certain about the summons to William's court, the archbishop would not receive justice. That bulwark of our modern justice, the independence of the judge upon his bench, was not yet known. The king's court literally belonged to the king, and in it the king, either in person or in the person of his nominee, presided. The judicial court of a Norman king was, as Palgrave expresses it, another name for the king's despotism. Rufus might think he now had the archbishop at his mercy. In a court of his own creation, on a plea which had to do with purely civil concerns, there could not possibly enter those side issues which had baffled all his earlier attacks, and there could be no verdict except one.

Anselm saw the situation and was weary of the whole matter. His position had long been difficult, this last weight made the burden intolerable. He asked for leave to go to Rome. When the request was presented, William jeered at it with a jibe which unconsciously hid a compliment to the man he was tormenting. "Why should *he* wish to go to Rome? He can have no sins which none but a pope can forgive. And if what he wants is advice, Urban is more likely to need Anselm's counsel, than Anselm Urban's." Anselm however was in no mood to be put aside with jests. When the request was refused at the Pentecost court of Windsor in 1097, he renewed it in August to be told that a petition of such gravity could not be determined off-hand by the king but must come before the great council of the realm. So the question between king and primate came before the court at Winchester

October 1097. The king had silently let fall the complaint about the archbishop's contingent, and the issue was clear.

Again the king refused Anselm's request, and added the warning that, if the demand were persisted in, he counted it sufficient reason for taking possession of the property of the see. The archbishop summoned his suffragans in order to lay the case before them. Careful to avoid all appearance of a cabal, they informed the king of the request, but they came. Their primate began to speak of the duties which lay on himself and them as bishops of the Church of Christ. Thereupon Walchelin of Winchester in name of his brethren begged him to look at the question from their point of view. The primate was alone, a stranger, a monk, he could afford to regard everything from a peculiarly high standpoint. But they could not afford to do this. They had affairs of this world in which they were interested, friends and dependants who looked to them for support. In even the highest matters they could not afford to ignore these considerations. If the plea was urged in all seriousness, it is a proof of the low estate into which the episcopate in England had sunk. But one suspects that there was a touch of irony in it, which the monkish chronicler failed to see, and that Walchelin meant to suggest to his superior how a man loses foothold on the solid earth through the pursuit of phantoms. Anselm accepted it literally. "Go," he said, "to your master, I will hold to my God."

The court party had one strong ground against Anselm's claim in the ancient customs of the kingdom. If the Primate of England without due cause shown

could leave his post and compel the king to grant a pass-
port for resort to Rome, the customs were broken.   Yet
these time-honoured customs the archbishop had sworn
to obey, when he made his compact with Rufus.   Anselm
could not but acknowledge the fact, but he added that
he had sworn obedience to those customs, so far as they
were consistent with justice and with the will of God.
No, said his opponents with one voice, the oath was
absolute and was taken with no such reservations.
Surely, the archbishop retorted, if such a reservation
was not expressly stated, it was at least implied.   Such
a reservation is and must be implied in every oath.
"No Christian man can bind himself to customs which
are opposed to the divine law.   It is, you say, contrary
to those customs of your realm that for the salvation
of my soul and the administration of the Church I
should visit St. Peter in his successor.   Such customs
are against God and worthy of condemnation."

That was something of an evasion.   It was the
business of the archbishop to have considered these
things before he took the oath, and if he found the
customs incompatible with what he regarded as his
duty to have declined the oath.   Anselm felt the
difficulty of his position, for, seated in the king's
presence, he proceeded to elaborate the question and to
lay down the necessary limitations which attach to
every oath.   But the king and the barons broke in
upon his statement.   This, they cried, is no argument,
it is a sermon.   When the clamour died down, Anselm
brought the whole question to an issue.   "You wish
me to swear never again to appeal to St. Peter or to
his vicar.   Such a demand no Christian ought ever to
make.   To take such an oath is to forswear St. Peter,

and to forswear St. Peter is to forswear Christ, who
made the apostle chief over His Church.   When I deny
Christ, I will readily pay the penalty in your court for
demanding this license."

The argument is unanswerable from Anselm's point
of view and from that of all who share its implied
conviction that the papal supremacy is of the essence
of Christianity and therefore any interference with it
touches conscience.   Hold it to be an essential part of
the law of Christ's Church on earth that each archbishop shall have free access to Rome and shall have
the right to determine for what cause he shall go, and
no oath will ever bind a Churchman to forego that right.
His conscience would have violence done to it by mere
earthly customs, if that were so.   But hold that only a
conscience which had been nurtured in the atmosphere
of Aosta and Le Bec could ever have thus construed
the essentials of Christianity, and then to set the
surrender of the right of appeal to Rome on the same
level as a denial of Christ will appear as one of the
means through which the papal system confuses the
moral issues of all questions and obscures the simplicities
of Christ.

The archbishop had been fully invested in his dignity.
He had accepted his benefice on the terms which were
then customary, the terms of becoming the king's liege
man and doing him homage.   He had been permitted
to exercise his authority, since he had consecrated other
bishops.   Liberty had been granted him to accept his
pallium from Pope Urban.   What he now required was
the recognition of a right which Lanfranc had never
exercised, which the Conqueror had never admitted, but
which the new claims of Rome were making appear

II

essential. It was a legitimate claim that England must consider that demand before admitting it, and should, if it were found out of harmony with her law, declare null the compact by which the archbishop held his property. To be forced into admitting the claim by an appeal to the archbishop's conscience was impossible. No one man's conscience can determine English law.

Anselm based his demand on opinions about the papal authority which no one in the king's court was prepared to deny. Laymen and clergy alike granted the pope's authority over the Church and the consequent duty on the part of each archbishop to obey that authority. But the king also had his claims over the archbishop, and in recognition of these the primate had sworn to his oath of allegiance. Was Rome at liberty without consulting the king to insist upon new demands which conflicted with the terms of that oath, and was every bishop to be at liberty to set aside the king's claim by pleading that obedience to Rome involved a question of conscience, which he dared not without peril to his soul ignore? In that case the liberties of all England and the obedience of all bishops to the civil power lay at the mercy of a foreign potentate, who without regard to England's interests might interfere materially with its prosperity and peace. It was with a wholesome sense of the independence of their island kingdom that all men in England now forsook their archbishop. At Rockingham they had supported him against the royal tyranny; at Winchester they refused to support him in denying the royal rights. "Go then to the pope," cried Robert of Meulan, speaking for Rufus' cabinet; "there remains to us what we know." Since the compact of his oath was broken, the property of the see was forfeit to the Crown.

Anselm turned to leave; he was already on his way to Canterbury, when he bethought him of all which his decision involved. He returned, re-entered the royal court, and stood before Rufus. "I am going, my lord," he said. "Had I gone with your goodwill, I judge it had become you better and had better pleased all good folk. As matters have not gone thus, on your account I regret it, for myself I will bear it quietly, and in spite of it will not surrender my love for your soul's welfare. And as one who knows not when he may see you again I commend you to God, and alike as a spiritual father to his beloved son, as the archbishop to the king, I desire, if you reject it not, to give you God's blessing and my own." "And I," the king answered, "do not refuse thy blessing." Over Rufus' bent head Anselm made the sign of the cross. It was their last meeting, October 15 1097.

For Anselm there remained the leave-taking with his monks. Anxiously he told them how he recognised that his was the easier task. Of late years matters had gone more pleasantly with them, because the archbishop had been present to stand between them and the king; but now the king would have them at his mercy and he would not spare. Yet they were no tyros in the school of Christ, and had long known that His school was one of trial. Let them but endure unto the end and so be saved.

Taking scrip and staff from the altar, the archbishop made his way to Dover. Here a last wanton insult from the king awaited him. No sooner was the

scene at Winchester over than Rufus seized the archiepiscopal revenues.   He bade Anselm leave the kingdom
but take nothing with him which belonged to it.   "I
have horses, clothing, books, does he mean these?   For
the want of these will not prevent me from going even
naked and barefooted to Rome."   "I do not mean
these things," was the curt reply.   "Let him go on his
way, and before he has left the kingdom he will learn
my meaning."   That meaning Anselm learned at Dover.
The royal clerk, William of Warelwast, was waiting
there.   He dined at the archbishop's table throughout
the fortnight during which adverse winds made it
impossible to cross the Channel.   On the last day he
presented himself on the beach, and in the king's name
demanded liberty to search all the baggage.   The
cynical publicity of the insult was characteristic of
Rufus.

# CHAPTER IX

## The First Exile and "Cur Deus Homo"

Landing at Wissant in November 1097, Anselm with his two companions, Baldwin of Tournay and Eadmer, avoided the territory of Normandy which was in Rufus' power, and made his way southward by Flanders and the France of that period. Here his person was revered and his work known; he was welcomed in every town by crowds which thronged to greet the venerable archbishop. The fact that he had held his own against the redoubtable King of England lent their visitor a peculiar honour in the eyes of the burghers. There is no stronger foe to a despotism than a victim whom it has been able to harass but unable to crush. The very presence of the man must have sent new thoughts of liberty into the minds of those corporations which, already conscious of their power, were beginning to think how they might use it. Specially welcome was the visitor in the monasteries where the principles of reform and the canons of Clermont council found their support. The monks reverenced in him the defender of the Catholic faith and the champion of the liberties of the Church. It was an honour to the monastery of St. Bertin that he consecrated an altar there to

St. Laurence, it was a pride to the citizens of St. Omer that their children received confirmation at his hands.

From one religious house to another the pilgrim passed through Burgundy until Cluny was reached in safety. The monastery was the fountainhead of reform. Christmastide was spent in the society of Hugh, its famous abbot, who had numbered among his monks both Hildebrand and Urban, whom the former had sent as legate to Hungary and the latter still honoured with his confidence. Hugh remained abbot at Cluny; there are men who prefer to inspire those who sit on thrones rather than be themselves hampered by the royal robes. From Cluny Anselm proceeded to Lyons. There, as archbishop of the city and ecclesiastical leader of the present France, ruled another Hugh. Hildebrand on his deathbed had nominated this former fellow-monk at Cluny as one of his possible successors on the papal chair; Victor had found it necessary to excommunicate him; Urban had found it equally necessary to restore him. One of the clearest heads in the tangled Church politics of that century and one of the most uncompromising, he had long been acquainted by letter with Anselm, while the latter was abbot of Le Bec. The two men had learned to respect each the other's character. Hugh welcomed his friend heartily, and in return for the quondam abbot's instruction in theology was able to initiate him into Church politics.

The result must have been an unwelcome surprise to the gentle archbishop. In England the papal power had risen before him in beautiful vision; in Lyons it appeared in its reality. The supreme pontiff, who ruled the Church for the ends of Christ and who gave speedy remedy to every wrong, gave place to the bishop of Rome holding uncertain footing in his own city, needing to veer with the change of circumstances, to attempt the possible rather than seek after the ideal. Hugh could show him things as they were. No one knew them better, the Rome in which the pope was never safe from insult, Northern Italy divided between his followers and those of the anti-pope, Southern Italy occupied by Normans who, intent on carving out for themselves a kingdom, were prepared to sell their swords to the highest bidder, Germany racked by intestine feuds which Urban must alternately foment and allay. Anselm began to see that in escaping from England to Rome he had not fled from the whirl of earthly business for which he felt himself unfit, but had merely involved himself in it more hopelessly. In the hour of disillusionment he wrote to the pope: "In the archbishopric during my four years I have brought forth no fruit, but have lived uselessly in great and dreadful troubles of spirit, so that to-day I would rather choose to die beyond England than to live in it. For, if I should require to finish my life there in the way in which I was living it, I foresee rather the damnation than the salvation of my soul." Refraining with simple mag-nanimity from any railings against his enemies, he put the state of affairs in England from his own point of view, and recounted the mental and moral dis-abilities which made him despair of being ever able to bring matters to a good issue, and finally in justice to the office, to England, and to himself, he begged Urban to relieve him of the duties. The answer was a distinct refusal and a summons to the imperial city.

The journey to Rome was, however, no easy task. The supporters of the antipope Wibert had a strong grasp on the north of Italy, and to them the capture of this important adherent of Urban would have been peculiarly grateful. The troubles of the time had also let loose all the forces of disorder. Robber bands were frequent, and to them a Churchman was no more than an ill-defended prize. Yet there was no help for it. In March 1098 Anselm, already a man of sixty-four, set out to cross the Alps by the well-remembered route, along which he had once gone into the world to seek for truth. He was coming back in search of justice, now one of the most famous figures in the west of Europe, but with well-nigh the same scant retinue. The Englishman Eadmer seems to have been charmed by the spice of adventure in the journey. His all too brief account of the episode gives a gracious idea of the *camaraderie* and innocent newsmongering which prevailed among the mediæval monasteries. To Anselm and his brethren the convent was the necessary terminus of the day's travel, not only because it gave them a lodging for the night and their daily bread, but because it offered the opportunity of that daily divine service which their Benedictine rule enjoined, and which habit had made as necessary to them as their daily bread. To the brethren in the monastery the arrival of strangers on the way to Rome was an opportunity for exercising the grace of hospitality and a welcome chance of learning something from the outer world.

Eadmer delightedly recounts how the abbot in one

convent warned them not to go on because even the
Archbishop of England had been obliged to turn back
from Piacenza and was now living in Lyons, and how
another, when he learned that some of his visitors had
made their profession in Le Bec, asked eagerly how
Anselm that man of God fared. That Anselm had
become an archbishop the abbot knew, but counted of
little importance. What he desired to learn was how
his brother fared in the travail of this life, because for
his part he prayed each day that it might be well with
his spirit. Among the barbarous struggles of the
time, in the country where Guelf and Ghibelline were
soon to divide every city and often to forget in their
feuds the very aims for which they fought, it is
charming to catch a glimpse of this apostolic picture
of a brotherhood in the one spirit. Not a little of
the Christian life was maintained and transmitted
across those centuries by the monasteries which did
not count Guelf and Ghibelline of chief importance,
and which prayed for each other's welfare in the
Lord.

On his arrival in Rome the archbishop was received
with high honour. Rooms were set apart for him in
the Lateran, where Urban then lived : the antipope
still held the Castle of St. Angelo. The day after his
coming he was received in solemn audience. A special
seat was placed for him beside the pope's chair. He
was acknowledged as the teacher from whom Urban
as well as all Christendom might be proud to learn.
But special praise was given to the humility which had
prompted one who stood so high in position and attain-
ments to recognise to the full Rome's claims. The
higher Urban set his new guest, the higher stood the

honour of the chair of St. Peter to which even that
guest bowed. There was policy as well as generosity
in the warmth of the welcome. Urban never forgot in
connection with Anselm that he was a useful pawn in
the game of asserting his own position against antipope and emperor. But Rome gave no real help. It
is true that the pope gave a formal hearing to the
archbishop's complaint against Rufus, that he acknowledged its justice, and in terms of this new view
of the situation wrote a letter to the King of England, bidding him restore Anselm to his dignities.
What more could even Rome do at that time? Urban
was engrossed in his favourite scheme of the Crusade, and in the negotiations for the reunion of the
Eastern and Western Churches which the Crusade had
brought anew to the front. He recognised more clearly
than Anselm's partisans could be expected to do the
futility of launching an excommunication against
Rufus. The King of England would not greatly care
about any excommunication. He might go cheerily
over to the acknowledgment of Wibert, or might
resolve that England could do very well without any
pope at all. An excommunication would have been
the assertion of a great principle. But Urban was no
Hildebrand, he did not realise the power over even
the most indifferent which comes from the bold assertion of a principle. It would be futile, would bring
Anselm no immediate advantage, might make more
difficult the position of the pope. Accordingly the
archbishop had to content himself with good words.
Letters passed between Rome and England. The
secretaries at the royal and papal courts were kept
more busy. Eadmer suggests that money came out of

satisfaction must also be rendered by man, since man has committed the offence and incurred the debt. Yet no man can render due satisfaction, for the debt is practically infinite, and nothing which a finite being can render is commensurate with it. Besides man, if he be considered as a creature, has nothing to offer to God which is not already due by the creature to his Creator. A perfect service is all which man *can* render, and a perfect service is what each man already owes to Almighty God.

The satisfaction must therefore be offered by one who, while man and therefore able to stand in man's place, is yet able to offer to God that which is of infinite value, and something which is not already due on his own part to God. In this light and from this point of view Anselm construes the Humiliation and the Passion. Christ, because He became man, became also able to render a deed and an obedience which could be offered for man. Because Christ was also God, what He wrought was of infinite worth. But Christ did not merely render a life of perfect obedience. That was no more than His due to God, so far as He had become man and submitted to man's limitations. Therefore He further surrendered Himself to death, a death which was in no wise His due, since by no sin had He brought it on Himself. This deed, which is so great because of the character of Him who wrought it that it merits an infinite recognition, merited its reward from His Father. Since, however, there is nothing by which God can add to the blessedness of His Son, Christ surrenders the reward to His brother men. It becomes the store of infinite merit which makes their salvation possible.

It is noteworthy in connection with the final sentences that Anselm nowhere, as later perverters of his doctrine have not hesitated to do, represents God as inflicting any punishment upon Christ. He lays peculiar emphasis on the voluntary character of Christ's sufferings, elaborately and with strained exegesis explains passages of Scripture which are tolerant of the opposite construction, and emphatically states that Christ met His death at the hands of the Jews because of His steadfast adherence to righteousness. But while the theory was not open to the perversions which it has thus suffered in many popular adaptations, it certainly did set the passion apart from the humiliation, regarded the latter as necessary only to qualify Christ for conveying His benefits to men, and made the passion as passion to be that by which alone the redemption of man is wrought.

The theory which Anselm framed has had a powerful influence directly and indirectly, and its indirect influence can be traced even where its conclusions are refused a formal reception. When the Church has refused to accept that idea of Christ's salvation, it has often retained the conception of God's relation to men from which the other sprang and which it helped to confirm. For the weakness of the whole position is the legality through which it construes all God's dealings with men. Sin is misunderstood when it is made synonymous with debt, and, since the obligations of conscience cannot be adequately represented as debt, since personal self-surrender is something essentially different from and richer than the nice calculation of all that is due to God's honour, the theory fails to interpret and therefore to educate the moral nature, and fails even more completely to represent the soul's hunger for the living God. I can transfer an obligation of the purse; I cannot transfer an obligation of the conscience. If I try to do it, I only hurt the conscience. If I think I have succeeded, that is a sign of a blunted conscience. Another may pay the debt which a man has contracted, and the creditor will not too carefully ask whence comes the money which he gladly accepts. But no one can fulfil the obligation, the very essence of which is that it rests on one man's conscience, must be recognised in that man's life, and must be fulfilled, if at all, by that man's patience.

Hence throughout the *Cur Deus Homo* the reader is cramped by the quantitative measures which Anselm applies to questions of morals. When he calculates the number of the redeemed which will be necessary and sufficient to make up for the number of the fallen angels, it is inevitable to remember that souls are hardly to be numbered like sheep. When he reckons the exact amount of satisfaction which will be required to make up for human transgression, it is a relief to realise that some things are beyond the power of the finest hair-balances. And when the infinite guilt which those who slew Christ brought upon themselves by their deed is spoken of as though it might possibly exhaust the infinite merit of the Saviour's death and thus leave nothing over which could be applied to the benefit of other souls, the impression deepens that a species of reckoning is introduced which in a region of this description is not at all at home, and the application of which can only produce confusion.

It is the same externalism of relation between God

12

and man which weakens the theory as a representation of what Christ is to the human spirit. Its inevitable tendency is to empty forgiveness of its ethical and spiritual significance. All men are shut up to this condition of condemnation because of a debt which they cannot and will never be able to pay. Christ has paid that debt to the full. There cannot be any real forgiveness when a debt has been fully paid. There is consequently no real meaning in the Divine grace. The Divine grace has accepted payment, and is no more grace. Divine grace prompted the payment, but thus grace is removed from the act of forgiveness, where in reality the soul is most conscious of it. Christ, because He has paid that debt, has made salvation possible to all men. How then does any individual soul come to partake in the benefits of this salvation? There remains nothing more than that the individual soul should come to understand the Divine arrangement, should recognise that this applies to itself, and should acquiesce in it. Faith accordingly becomes almost entirely an intellectual act of appreciation and acquiescence, and is emptied of most of its moral and spiritual content.

The weight in the great work of redemption was thrown, not on the moral condition of the recipient who was tested by that appeal, and grew through his answer to it. The weight was thrown on the external application of an external help. The theory accordingly tended to make Christ outward and not inward, an arrangement made to satisfy the Divine requirements. Now to externalise Christ is to externalise all the means of grace. Men who find it possible to think of Christ in these terms find it equally possible

to conceive His grace as ministered through the con-
tingencies of clerical orders and limited by the acci-
dents of a formal ritual.   To conceive of Christ as an
arrangement is to lose sooner or later the spiritual
sense of Sacrament and Church.   Christ had wrought
the great deed through which the store of merit was
laid up on behalf of sinful mankind.   The Church
became the means through which the arrangement
was intimated and by which the store was dispensed.
The Church was present to minister the benefits of
Christ to the souls of all who were within its reach.
But the faith which appropriates Christ, the inward
self-surrender through which Himself and the spirit
who loves Him become one in aim and hope, and which
thus becomes the source of a new moral and spiritual
life, was more and more thrust into the background.
Anselm's own religious life was fed from deeper
springs than his theory recognised, but that does not
make it the less true that his theory was one more
influence which helped in time to materialise and
externalise the mediæval Church.

This result has been inevitable from the ultimate
principle of the theory.   It offers no starting-point for
the new moral life which springs out of living contact
with Christ, and can offer no adequate explanation of
the Christian facts of experience.   On the theory,
in order that the soul may receive the benefits of
Christ's atoning work, there is no need of any moral
relation to Christ.   When the statement was accepted
in a modified form by another school of theologians
and transplanted into a very different soil, men sought
to supply the needed point of attachment by gratitude.
Because of all which Christ has wrought for  man's

salvation, and in thankful acknowledgment of all that
has come and will come from His passion and death,
the soul rises up to walk in newness of life.    And
when that life grows uncertain, the spirit turns back to
remember what it has received, and to quicken its
flagging zeal by the memory of its great debt.    Yet
this emotion is not the means through which the benefit is conveyed: it is the sign that the gift has already
been accepted.    It presupposes the benefit as already
received, and for that very reason cannot become the
channel of its reception.

And further, the theory does not correspond to the
religious facts.    It offers an inaccurate and wholly
inadequate idea of the relation between the soul of the
Christian and his Redeemer.    That relation is much
richer in content than the idea of past deeds of tenderness can ever convey.    It is significant in this connection that Anselm the writer of *Cur Deus Homo*
and Anselm the author of *Prayers and Meditations*
are two.    The theory as to redemption which he has
elaborated in his treatise does not find any vital place
in his *Meditations*.    When he speaks and writes of the
facts of the religious life in his own soul, he includes
elements for which his theory cannot account, states
conditions which that is compelled to ignore, recognises
factors which have no right to be present.

But there is one commanding thought which domin-
ates the whole *Cur Deus Homo*, as it dominated the
whole life of the author, and this was his most significant contribution to the question.    To Anselm the wide
universe with all it holds or ever will hold is nothing
except the mirror in which God manifests Himself.    It
has come into being and continues in being for no other

end save to represent the thought of Him who made it. Except so far as it does manifest God, it has neither meaning nor purpose. That is what makes it an ordered world—a cosmos and not a chaos. Because man is the crown of this creation, because in virtue of his being a rational intelligent creature he is that in which the otherwise unspoken purpose of this world comes to expression, his sin does not and cannot concern himself alone. It affects the whole world. It threatens to destroy its very purpose. It is in a real sense an effort to undo God's act in creation, because it threatens to undo the end which God had before Him when He created the world. This, to our mind, is Anselm's idea of the " honour of God." Sin would dethrone God, inasmuch as it threatens, in turning man aside from his true end, to pervert the whole purpose of God's world from what God Himself intended when He called it into being.

It is therefore impossible that God should pass by sin as though it were nothing. If He should do so, it would mean that He were content that His counsel should be thwarted. And God does not pass by sin. Since He has so far limited Himself as to permit a free will with all its awful privilege to exist alongside of His own, He can only assert His honour by punishment. Punishment to Anselm is not revenge, it is not even the means used for the improvement of the offender and justified by the resultant improvement in the offender. He has seen more deeply into it than that. Punishment is the assertion of God's purpose in an individual or a community which refuses to accept that purpose willingly, but which cannot remove itself outside the scope of the Divine decree, and which must therefore submit, however unwillingly, to that purpose. Further, God cannot accept back on its mere repentance the soul which has sinned. That He should do so seems to Anselm to mean that He puts this soul into the same position as though it had never sinned. He gives to that spirit as much as He could have given to the soul which had never departed from Him. That He should thus by an "arbitrary act of mercy" remit the penalty seems to Anselm to make possible the idea that the penalty was also arbitrary, and that the law of right-eousness is liable to change. There must be some satisfaction to this honour of God, some proof signal and awful that the law of righteousness was as un-changeable as God's being, and was in fact the very nature of God Himself. Man could not make such satisfaction. Anselm knew from his own experience and from the experience of the Church that Christ did. He knew the fact which, explain it how men will, is the core of the Church's sense of guilt and relief, that Christ and Christ only can relieve the conscience of its intolerable burden, and yet leave the moral law in all its unsullied majesty within the conscience. And the Church will ever owe a debt of gratitude to the man who with no forerunner along that dim and perilous way expressed this ultimate fact of its experience in so incisive a form that it could never again be ignored.

Anselm spoke to his time in language which his time could understand. The idea of God as a moral governor, whose demands on men are as inevitable and as un-changeable as His being, was one which his age needed. The language in which it was expressed may be felt to be inadequate and even misleading, but it might have passed unheeded, if it had been otherwise expressed.

And what is its final sense under any language was the truth which sustained the man's fine courage and indomitable patience. God was holy and, unless He ceased to be God, could not fail to require holiness alike from His subjects and His sons. It was the fresh recognition of that truth which was giving hundreds of men in Benedictine monasteries desire and courage to lay strong hands on their own lusts and discipline to finer issues their wayward and rebellious wills. It was the recognition of that truth which was nerving the better spirits of the mediæval Church to speak and act for the ends of Christ. At the court of the brutal Rufus Anselm had stood, and he was yet to stand before the wily Beauclerk, in the name of One who was greater than they. Behind him was God. Above king and court and archbishop was the claim of that supreme law which no rebellion could ever alter and the penalties of which no neglect could hope to evade. God must be a strong tower or a rock of offence. There were but the two alternatives, and men must choose.

It was what those licentious, untamed barons needed to hear and see. It was the idea of God which they were capable of grasping. It was couched in language which even they could understand. Swift to exact their rights from those beneath them and jealous lest their honour should even in the smallest tittle be derogated from among their equals, they needed to be made to realise that there was One who would exact a like honour from them and who would exact it to the uttermost. He and He alone could forego the demands of His own justice. To God and not to the easily quieted conscience, to God and not to the easily stilled remorse of heart belongeth mercy. The very limitations of Anselm's statement may have aided the acceptance of his thought. He spoke in terms which his contemporaries could understand. The theory suited an age which conceived and could only conceive sin as the violation of an external law.

An interesting historical parallel might be drawn in this respect between the thought of Anselm and that of Calvin. In an age which had rediscovered the desirability of the appetites and found little moral support or guidance in the outward forms of society, Calvin also stood forward to insist upon the decrees of God which are His eternal purpose. And to the Reformers as to Anselm the possibility of forgiveness and the reality of the Atonement became a burning question.

# CHAPTER X

## COUNCILS OF BARI AND ROME

IN the late summer of 1098 the pope visited Southern
Italy. Not the least of his many cares was the endeavour to retain loyal to the holy see the Normans
of that district. These had left their homes as pilgrims, but were well content with the Jerusalem which
the south of Italy offered them. At one time they
were caressed as the true defenders of the Church:
among them Hildebrand secured peace to die. At
another time they set up in the semi-Byzantine
cathedral of Monreale near Palermo the figure of one
of their kings crowned by the Redeemer, as the public
sign that they required no recognition from the
sovereign pontiff. Dangerous but necessary allies were
the Southern Normans.

Anselm, invited to accompany the pope, made another
effort to be rid of his archbishopric. Whether the
monastic life had wound itself anew about his heart, or
his clearer understanding of the difficulties involved in
the whole situation made him hopeless of obtaining any
help from Rome, he begged Urban to relieve him from
the burden. But Urban had learned to know the man
better, and recognised that a vacancy in the see would
be to the advantage of Rufus. He meant to maintain

Anselm as a constant protest against the King of England's violation of ecclesiastical law and as a means of reopening the whole question when a more favourable opportunity presented itself. The pope accordingly made a strong appeal to the primate's sense of self-sacrifice, and commanded him not to flinch from the post of duty.

He further bade Anselm be present at a synod which was to be held at Bari on October 1, when the affairs of England would be considered along with much other business. More than 180 bishops were convened in the Church of St. Nicholas on that day, and among them appeared delegates from the Eastern Church. The Crusade had caused a *rapprochement* between the court of Constantinople and the courts of the West, and the possibility of an alliance between the courts had made more desirable the healing of the schism between the two branches of the Church. Urban was hopeful that he might use the Crusade to restore unity to the Church, and use both to strengthen his own position and crush his rival the antipope. At the council the Eastern bishops brought forward the difficulty their patriarch felt about acknowledging a Church which had added to the Nicene Creed and taught that the Holy Spirit proceeded both from Father and Son. The pope sought to justify his Church, but at last hardpressed called on Anselm who had seated himself among the crowd of bishops to arise for the defence of the faith. The unknown, about whose identity the whispering bishops asked each other, stepped forward and proffered the argument which he later elaborated into a treatise, *De Processione Spiritus Sancti contra Græcos.*

The pamphlet is lucid and subtle but, it must be confessed, lacks vitality. In that respect it shares the fate of the whole discussion. The real questions which kept the Eastern and Western Churches apart were questions of practical politics and administration, on the ecclesiastical side the claim of Rome to be supreme over the Greek patriarch, on the political side the relation between the rival emperors of Constantinople and the West. Each branch of the Church had had time and opportunity to develop an ethos of its own : each had developed a hierarchy which was jealous of its own dignity and incapable of appreciating any union which did not imply uniformity. When circumstances made it convenient for East and West to work together, the difference in dogma shrank into the background : when either section wished for other reasons to hold aloof from the other, the difference of dogma formed a convenient pretext for breaking off negotiations.

Anselm's treatise has the merit that it strove to lift the discussion to higher levels than those to which it frequently sank. The Greeks were in the habit of pressing their formal advantage, and of insisting that, whether legitimate or illegitimate in itself, the *filioque* was an unwarranted addition to the original Nicene Creed. The Romans sought to escape from the charge of innovation by showing that the clause was not an absolute novelty, but was implied at least in certain authoritative pronouncements from the early centuries, and taught by some among the Fathers whom both East and West recognised. The discussion frequently sank to that barren type which transforms theology into a branch of archæology. Anselm however insisted that the Western addition, though it was not embodied in the Nicene formula, was implied in the Trinitarian dogma. It was the inevitable and necessary elaboration of what is already implied in the doctrine that the Son is homo-ousios or of the same nature as the Father. The Spirit proceeds from the Father, not so far as He is Father, but so far as He is God. But everything which can be predicated of the Father can equally be predicated of the Son, except that which is peculiar to the Father as Father. Since the Spirit proceeds from the Father, so far as He is God and not so far as He is Father, the Spirit proceeds from that in the Divine nature which is common to the Father and the Son. He must therefore proceed from the Son also. The Father and the Son are one, not merely alike but one in essence. Whatever then can be predicated of either of these, not in His separate relation as Father or as Son, but in the essence of the Godhead which is common to both, must be predicable of the other also. To teach otherwise is to obscure the identity which exists between Father and Son, to be homoiousian and not homo-ousian. The Greeks, Anselm insisted, had not thoroughly mastered the teaching of Athanasius, and were still involved, if not in the principles, at least in the consequences of the Arian heresy.

At the close of the council Urban laid before the assembled bishops the position of Anselm, and after a review of affairs in England demanded the advice of his brethren. They gave it that, since the king had been sufficiently warned, the Church must now proceed to the final act of judgment and excommunicate its contumacious son. Urban expressed his agreement and his intention so to proceed. But Anselm threw himself at the pope's feet and prayed for mercy. With apparent reluctance Urban consented to a further delay. The scene has an air of theatrical unreality. At that very time Urban knew that messengers were on their way from England with letters from Rufus. Till these arrived, it was impossible to tell whether the king was contumacious or not. To condemn a man for contumacy with his letters unread was an absurdity.

The messengers reached Rome when Urban and Anselm had returned to the city for the winter. One announced that, while Rufus had consented to read the pope's letter, he had not only refused to take any message from his archbishop, but had sworn that its monkish bearer must leave the kingdom immediately on peril of having his eyes torn out. Behind these came William of Warelwast with the royal answer. In a public audience Urban extracted from the envoy the admission that the king's sole ground of complaint against his archbishop was that the latter had insisted in defiance of the royal will on liberty to plead his cause at Rome. The pope bade the man note the absurdity of coming to Rome itself in order to present such a complaint. The imperturbable chaplain however requested a private audience. He had money and influence enough to make friends for his master's cause about the person of the pope. William of Malmesbury declares roundly that the pope himself was bribed. The result at least was that, though now the contumacy was proved beyond a doubt, a delay for nine months was granted to Rufus. Anselm grew weary of seeing the confiscated revenues of his archbishopric used to pervert Roman justice. He asked leave to go, but was bid remain until the Easter synod.

At this which was held in Rome and attended by one hundred and fifty bishops the chief questions dealt with referred to discipline. Several canons were passed to define the meaning of lay investiture. Anathema was pronounced against all laymen who gave staff and ring, against all clerics who received investiture at the hands of laymen, against all bishops consecrating clergy who accepted investiture from laymen. A like anathema was levelled against every man who in order to attain a spiritual office did homage to a layman. "It was," so Eadmer represents Urban to have said, "a thing execrable to see hands which are summoned to a supreme honour such as even the angels themselves do not share, the honour of creating by their ministrations God the Creator of all things in order to present Him as a sacrifice before God the Father for the redemption and salvation of all the world, reduced to the degradation of becoming the slaves of hands which night and day are defiled by impurity and rapine and are dipped in blood." It might be as the pope averred, but it was what Anselm and every bishop in England had done without hesitation and without scruple. Apart from that stupendous claim for the clergy, the Church could not expect the State to surrender homage without a severe struggle. The form by which the bishop became the king's man was of slight importance, the fact was too important to be lightly given up. If the bishops were to continue to be great lords, they must continue to acknowledge the duties which their lordship implied. An immunity of this character meant the introduction of confusion into every kingdom. The only logical result was that, if

the bishops desired to be free from the obligations
implied in homage, they must give up the privileges
which made them liable to those obligations. They
must surrender their estates and their high civil
functions. If they were unwilling to do this, they
could not, because they were Churchmen, legislate
themselves out of the just payment of the duties which
their privileges required from them.

The council was marked by a dramatic incident.
The sittings were held in the Church of St. Peter.
Since the church was open to the pilgrims who went
and came to the grave of the chief apostle, it was
difficult for anyone who read the canons before the
assembly for their confirmation to make his voice
heard by all. A certain Reinger, bishop of Lucca,
who possessed a clear ringing voice was selected to
read from the ambo. Hardly however had he gone
far before he stopped short, and, when men startled
by the silence looked up, burst out: "What are we
doing here? We are laying laws on the compliant,
and failing to resist the rebellious. To this place come
the complaints of the distressed: from this as supreme
head counsel and help are expected. Yet all the world
sees the result. One sits among us, who has come
from the world's end, patient, meek, silent. But his very
silence is his loudest outcry. . . . This one, I repeat,
has come hither under the burden of a cruel wrong,
to seek justice from the apostolic see. He has been
two years here, and what succour has he found? If
you do not all know whom I mean, I mean Anselm,
archbishop of England." Those were days when men
counted themselves not the less loyal to the Roman
see, though they spoke about its failure in duty.

There was no conspiracy of silence then. Reinger's staff fell ringing on the pavement, his breath panted under his vehement outburst. "Brother," said the pope, "it is enough. We shall take heed to this matter." Reinger was not yet content. "Good need is there that heed be given. Else must we remember that there is a higher tribunal which shall judge even our judgment."

On the following day, Eadmer adds with unconscious irony, "having obtained permission we left Rome, and we received no more of counsel or of justice through the Roman bishop than I have mentioned." The visit to Rome had been a disappointment to Anselm and his friends. He had not been permitted to retire from office, nor received such a measure of support in it as would have spared him the necessity of taking a vigorous part himself.

Returning to Lyons, Anselm was received with high honour. Hugh was not unwilling to entrust some of the cares of his archdiocese to a man whom he could wholly trust. No great fête-day was counted complete without the stranger's presence. No church could be duly consecrated without his benediction. Especially did many throng to receive his instructions for their confirmation. The man had the rare gift of speaking with entire sincerity on religious truths. And the work appealed to him, for, Eadmer states, though we who assisted him were wearied to death by the duty, he was never more content than when he was busied about the task of strengthening the souls of men.

Inevitably in that age the idea of miraculous power gathered round the figure of the saintly archbishop.

Men believed he was nearer the Source of all health both to body and soul than they. One illustration will suffice to show the popular belief and Anselm's attitude to it. Two men, knights and gentlemen, whose appearance showed them to be the victims of low fever, arrived one day when the archbishop was at table. Coming before him they begged a crust from his hands. Anselm, who saw from their dress that their request did not arise from poverty and who suspected their real design, refused the crust but invited them to take their places at the table. One of the monks however, who had more compassion or fewer scruples, handed them a fragment which his master's hand had already touched. They accepted it, and after the meal drew Eadmer aside, and asked him to help them in their desire to receive the sacrament at Mass from the hands of the saint. "We desire it in order that we may be freed from intolerable bodily pains which we suffer. It may be however that this bread will relieve us. If so we shall not come to the Mass. And our absence will be a sign to you that we are already cured." Eadmer promised to obtain for them what they wished, but when they did not appear concluded that the table crust had procured the desired effect. The archbishop believed as simply as every man in his period did that miraculous power might be bestowed on any true servant of God. He could be no stranger to the fact that men regarded him as possessed of such power, but he was too unsparing a student of his own heart not to realise the danger of spiritual pride which the belief in his own endowment with it was liable to foster in the heart of every man, and he was further of too spiritual a

13

vision not to see the dangers which attend a craving after the sensational and the wonderful. He realised the risk of superstition, when men sought the sacrament to be cured from ague, and when the ague was cured went home without the sacrament. While other men recounted tales about his unconscious deeds, he gravely discouraged all speech concerning them.

In works of mercy and duty and in the composition of another treatise, *De Conceptione Virginali et Peccato Originali*, the months of exile wore away. But, while all was quiet in Lyons, events were following fast on each other outside. On the 29th of July 1099 Urban died, within a fortnight of the fall of Jerusalem which he had done so much to free and of the recovery of which he was not to hear. On August 13 the conclave appointed a former monk of Cluny, whom Hildebrand had made a cardinal, to be Pope Paschal II. When Rufus heard the news of Urban's death, "God's hate," he said, "fall on him who cares. But what sort of man is his successor?" "A man not unlike Anselm," he was told. "By the face of God then he is of no use. But he may look to his own business. His popedom will not get the better of me. I am free now and mean to keep my freedom." He used the opportunity to make one effort at treating with Anselm without the intervention of Rome, but the terms he offered were trifling. Anselm was compelled to refuse them and to write a long letter to Paschal in which he stated his case anew and requested that he might not be sent back to England, unless he were empowered to demand new terms from the king.

There was however to be another solution to the quarrel between these two than any which Rome could supply. The Church in England had begun to look upon their king as fey. His oppression continued and even increased. He held in his power three vacant bishoprics and about twelve abbeys, he spent their revenues on his own ends. Men through very custom or through a superstitious dread had ceased to remonstrate, for a supernatural success appeared to attend the king. It was as though he could not fail. Once he was about to start on an expedition in England, when news reached him of troubles in Maine. He turned his horse, rode straight to the coast and bade some fishermen put to sea in the teeth of a Channel gale. They urged the danger, but Rufus cursed them in all lightness of heart and bade them call to mind whether they had ever heard of a king who was drowned. Even the sea became his servant, for no sooner had the boat been fairly pushed off than the wind changed. It was, Eadmer wrote, as though God desired to prove him. When the king rose from his sickbed near the beginning of the reign, he had sworn that God should never make him good by the evil He had given, and now God would prove whether limitless good could move him.

The accounts of the king's last years leave the curious impression that Rufus' arrogant blasphemy imposed on the imagination of his subjects until men watched with awe this drama of a struggle between the Almighty and one man's soul. The tension of their awe betrayed itself in the presages of the king's death which ran from lip to lip. In the monastery of St. Alban's which he had wantonly robbed a monk saw Anselm along with many English saints stand before the throne of God. All accused the king of

many wrongs done to Holy Church. The Almighty
addressed St. Alban, " Come nigh, thou glorious proto-
martyr of the English, avenge the saints of England,
whom a tyrant outrages." Thereon an arrow was
handed to the saint. He flung it down. " Take, O
Satan, all power over King William."

On August 2 1100 the king was found with an
arrow through his breast in the New Forest which
had been his father's pride and his people's hate, and
which had already proved so fatal to his race. The
Saxon chronicler with a grave reticent simplicity is
content to say, " He died in the midst of his unright-
eousness without repentance and without restitution."
Lascivious, brutal, blasphemous, knowing no law
higher than his own appetites he too helped to make
England. Without his dominant personality and
stubborn will the Heptarchy might have returned, a
Heptarchy of Norman nobles.

The news was brought to Anselm at Chaise Dieu
not far from Lyons. The monks wondered when they
saw the grave face, to which the dead man had
brought many heavy cares, bow between their master's
hands. He burst into tears and to their unexpressed
wonder gave answer, " I would rather have died
myself than that the king should have passed as he
has done."

# CHAPTER XI

ENGLAND was saved from confusion through the prompt action of Henry, the youngest son of the Conqueror. Beauclerk had learned in the school of experience to bide his time; he had also learned that when a man's opportunity has come he dare not wait to make up his mind about how he means to grasp it. Leaving others to bury his brother's body, he rode hard to Winchester and made himself master of the royal treasury. Yet he did not ride so hard but that William of Breteuil was in time to enter a protest on behalf of Robert, Duke of Normandy, then absent on crusading and matrimonial business. The protest served to quicken proceedings. Those of the barons of England who were present forthwith met in Witan and proclaimed Henry their elect lord. Within three days of Rufus' death the new king was consecrated to his office by Maurice, bishop of London. Yet the coronation, rapid though it was, was not effected before the king had pledged himself in a definite charter to undo the lawlessness of the last reign and restore the excellent customs of the Confessor. With equal emphasis Henry promised to restore liberty to the Church. The sense in which this liberty was understood could be gathered from the specific pledge, that vacancies of bishoprics and abbacies were no longer to be artificially prolonged in order that the king might enjoy their revenues.

Two of the earliest acts of the government showed the change which had come over affairs. Ranulf the Flambard, who had become bishop of Durham, whom men accounted the secret instigator and instrument of Rufus' worst acts of oppression, and whom Anselm in a rare lapse of temper called "that publican of the publicans," was stripped of all his offices and cast into the Tower. And before the coronation William Giffard was nominated to the vacant see of Winchester; now Giffard was above even the suspicion of simony.

These things promised well. Men noted however that the latest of the Norman kings, those mighty hunters before the Lord, held firmly to the hated forest-laws: they were soon to learn that, while the coarse tyranny exercised toward the clergy was at an end, the king's idea of the Church's legitimate liberty was not that of Rome. Beauclerk was no bully like his brother, nor did he merely hunger after the Church's revenues, but he was not the man to surrender a single prerogative of his crown. Disciplined in the school of misfortune, he had learned tenacity and the control of his passions. None the less was he the son of the Conqueror. Prudent, cunning, ambitious, he could temporise but only in order to avoid a surrender. He could play the barons against each other and the English folk against them all. The power of the Church, through its moral influence over the minds of men and its centralised organisation served by the best intelligence of the time, had not escaped one of the

acutest brains of that generation. Though his own
Churchmanship was of the politic sort more than that
of one who was personally devout, he was too shrewd
a man placed in too difficult circumstances to throw
so powerful an organisation into opposition; but he
was quite as resolved as his father " to have all the
croziers of England in his own hand."

There was need for all the new king's prudence.
The Norman kingship was too young to have become
consecrated by custom. The individual was still more
than the institution, needing to uphold it almost as
much as he was upheld by it. Each new possessor of
the dignity must prove himself fit to reign, before men
submitted to him. Robert too was on his way home,
with the glory won at the Crusades to aid him, with a
wealthy bride to supply funds. The Conqueror's eldest
son had never willingly submitted to the decision which
shut him out from the throne of England. It seemed
injustice that so fair a heritage should be denied to the
firstborn, and he meant to try a fall with his brother
before he acquiesced. Nor did Robert lack supporters
among the English barons. Some favoured him because they hoped for the license their friends in Normandy enjoyed under the easy duke, others invited
him because they possessed in addition to their English
property fiefs across the Channel. The latter reason
long made it difficult for two rulers to hold England
and Normandy, and was to become one cause which
impelled Beauclerk himself to Tinchebray ; at present
it brought his brother into his new dominion.

One of the king's earliest acts was to summon
Anselm. A letter arrived at Lyons, in which the
archbishop was begged to hasten his return. It con-

tained the assurance that only necessity of State had compelled the king to accept consecration from any other hand than his primate's, and that from this time Anselm's counsel should receive its due weight. Money to pay the traveller's expenses and debts would have been sent with the letter, had not the condition of Normandy made its transit insecure. For that reason the archbishop was advised to avoid the duchy and sail from Wissant. Messengers would bring money to Dover, and meantime the revenues of the see were at his command.

Anselm made such good speed that he landed at Dover on September 23. The two chief causes of his quarrel with Rufus were tacitly decided by the terms in which he was invited to return. There was to be no more filching of the archiepiscopal property for royal uses, and the Church in England received the right to hold free intercourse with the papal see. In the view of Englishmen and even of most English Churchmen it seemed that there was no ground for further quarrel.

Not long after Anselm's landing king and primate met at Salisbury. Beauclerk, after repeating his regret that the Archbishop of Canterbury had not been present to give the consecration, requested Anselm to do him homage for title, rights, and lands as he had done it to his brother. It has been said that this was a novel demand, for which there was no ground in English constitutional law. But, since Anselm did not repel the request on the ground of its novelty, the question in this connection is purely academic and may be left for experts in Norman legal procedure to determine. Although the demand was an unusual one, circumstances made it appear advisable. The king was uncertain which men within his realm he could trust. Not all his nobles were loyal to him, and he required the greatest and most independent of them all to set an example of loyal support to the rest. The request *may* have been exceptional, but so were the circumstances.

Anselm promptly but firmly refused. He stated the canons which Rome had laid down on the subject for the government of the Church. His objection was not against doing homage to Beauclerk, but against doing homage to any king. He had been present at, and had taken part in the decisions of councils which declared that anyone who offered homage or who accepted investiture from lay hands was excommunicate. That was the simple and sufficient reason why he could not do to Henry what he had done to his brother. Let the king clearly understand the situation. On no other terms than these could he consent to remain within the realm. If Henry was not prepared to submit to them, the primate must withdraw from the kingdom. Primarily the question between king and archbishop was that of homage. Anselm was required to render homage, not to accept investiture. But the other question was sure to emerge, so soon as the king invested a new bishop with staff and ring and sent him to the archbishop for consecration. If Anselm consecrated such a bishop, he made himself liable to Church censure. The two questions were inevitably bound up together, and the primate preferred to raise them both.

King and counsellors were startled by this statement, and, when it is remembered that the Church in England had been practically cut off from Rome during Anselm's three years of exile, it is easy to understand why the decision took them by surprise. This was a wholly new claim. All that the archbishop had demanded from Rufus had been freely granted by his successor, and the result was that the homage which the archbishop rendered to Rufus was refused to his successor. Henry however soon regained control of the situation, and asked that the whole matter might be hung up till Easter. Meantime he promised to despatch a messenger to the pope, to learn the exact scope of this new demand, to explain how it clashed with all the customs of England, and to inquire whether in the present position of affairs in the kingdom it could not be modified. There is no reason to suspect Henry's sincerity in making this request. His desire to avoid a quarrel with Anselm at this time may have been partly due to the wish not to lose the primate's moral support, but to say this is only to say that he tried to fulfil his duty to England. To anyone, however, who does not count it wickedness that any king measured the Church's claims before he granted them, the king's embarrassment before the unexpected situation and his sincere and unselfish admiration for the character of his great prelate are equally patent.

Anselm had no hesitation in consenting to a delay. He had no doubt as to the answer which would come back from Rome. He had gauged the vital importance of the whole question, and had had occasion to judge the temper of Rome in connection with it. There was little likelihood that the pope would resile from the position he had deliberately taken. But the primate knew the difficulty of Henry's position in England, and

though no Englishman he was too true a patriot to
his adopted country to make capital for his see out of
the political perplexities of the court at the risk of
making civil war possible in England.

The terms of a truce were arranged.    Anselm should
receive and administer his see with all the revenues
accruing to it as freely as had been the case in the days
of Lanfranc.    The king should appoint and invest
bishops to vacant sees.    But while the archbishop was
not to be required to consecrate the bishops who received investiture from the king, he was not to refuse
his communion to them nor to treat them as *ipso
facto* excommunicate.    If the answer from Rome were
unfavourable to the royal wishes, Anselm's position
would be unprejudiced.

During the period of truce events marched rapidly,
and Anselm had the opportunity to show his sagacious
loyalty alike to his king and to the best interests
of his adopted country.    The uncertain allegiance of
the Norman nobles had a result which affected profoundly the fate of England.    It threw Henry back
on the support of the English people.    Already the
fact that their new king was English-born had appealed to the singular pride of the insular race.    The
other sons of the Conqueror had been aliens to the
land, and were born to their father while he was
no more than Duke of Normandy.    This one had first
seen the light under an English sky, when his father
was already King of England.    Henry porphyrogeni-
tus was quick to see his advantage in the fact, and
sought to confirm his position by marrying Edith, the
daughter of Malcolm of Scotland and Margaret grand-
niece of Edward the Confessor.    The marriage was sure

to win the affection of the Saxons, who looked back
with foolish fondness to their last native king: it
would also define the king's future policy. But a grave
difficulty stood in the way. Edith had been trusted
for her education to the care of an aunt Christina,
abbess of Romsey in Hampshire. While the girl lived
in the convent the abbess had compelled her to wear
the veil in order to shield her from the insults of a
wanton court. There is a story of how Rufus once
found his way to the convent and went into its church
to say his prayers there. But the superior evidently
suspected her king's devotion, for she at once hurried
away to throw a veil over her dangerously beautiful
niece. Already however Rufus had penetrated into
the cloister and was enjoying the fresh scent of " the
roses and lilies of its garden." It is a little difficult to
realise Rufus walking in a nunnery garden and smelling
lilies, but one cannot doubt that the abbess knew the
character of her kinsmen, and the prompt action which
resulted from the knowledge throws a somewhat ugly
sidelight on the much vaunted chivalry of the century.

Malcolm had had no intention that his daughter should
" enter religion." He had very different intentions
about her future. Once when he found her wearing
the veil on the occasion of a visit to the convent, he had
torn the emblem from her head. Edith herself averred
that the dress had been forced on her by dint of hard
words and harder blows from her aunt. Whenever
she found herself unwatched, she had not hesitated to
tear the hated symbol and trample it under her young
and petulant feet. Yet the fact remained that she had
been seen veiled in the convent, and in those early
years in England no consecration service was counted

necessary at the cloistering of virgins. That a girl wore the veil was enough in the eyes of men to make her an oblate. It threatened therefore to cause a grave scandal if the king signalised his accession by making his wife one who was already accounted a bride of Christ.

The question was laid before the archbishop for his decision. He resolved it with the rare and simple courage which was characteristic of the man. If this thing were to be done, it should not be done in a corner, nor should it be effected by means of a papal dispensation with its suggestion of a large mulct paid for compliance, which left on men the hurtful impression that many of the ecclesiastical regulations were nothing more than means for the extortion of money. Anselm summoned a council of Churchmen and laymen to Lambeth and laid the case before them. Commissioners were sent to the convent who confirmed the truth of all Edith's assertions. The archbishop himself reminded the council that a precedent could be found in the days of Lanfranc, for that prelate had released from their vows a large number of Anglo-Saxon women who in the days of violence and blood after the Conquest had taken shelter within the convent walls, but who desired in later years to return to their duties in the world. If women who of their own choice had taken the vows could be released, much more could one who had worn the veil against her will. Left alone to arrive at their decision, the counsellors decided for Edith's liberty. Anselm returned to make himself jointly responsible for the resolution, declared his entire concurrence with their sentence, and refused Edith's offer to submit to any ordeal by which the truth of her statements might be tested.

And finally the archbishop declared the whole course of proceedings before an assembled throng at Westminster and called upon any who doubted its legality even now to interfere. When none spoke, he married Edith to King Henry on November 11 1100. He gave England its good Queen Maud, and won for himself a loyal and lifelong friend. The archbishop's action gave umbrage to the stricter party among the clergy, for John of Salisbury who wrote his Life in order to secure Anselm's canonisation carefully suppresses the whole incident. Nor was it a welcome thing for the insolent Normans to bend before a daughter of the conquered race. They sneered to the end at the royal pair and named them Godric and Godgifu, goodman and goody. But the marriage won for Henry a warmer place in the hearts of the English, and the English axes held the kingdom for him.

There was need, for Robert was now home from his crusading. The Flambard had made his escape from the Tower and joined him. Many were following that example, and more were only waiting for an opportunity to do the like. The Norman duke crossed the Channel and effected a landing. It is unnecessary to detail the negotiations, for matters never came to battle. The brothers seem to have been afraid to venture on the final push of pike. The king and duke met at Winchester; and Robert, having received the promise of an annual subsidy of 3000 silver marks, went home to spend it. But in the matter Anselm's character was of prime value in bringing about an arrangement between Henry and his subjects. Not only was his loyalty to the king of great moral weight, but the trust men reposed in his honour made him an invaluable negotiator between the mutually distrustful parties. Eadmer says bluntly that Anselm saved the crown to the king, and though no other puts the matter with the same force, there can be little doubt that Henry gained considerable support from the undeviating loyalty of his archbishop.

These events and the failure of Henry's messenger to return at Easter had delayed, but between two such opponents could only delay, the ecclesiastical question. For those who had now met were men fully capable of realising the magnitude of the debate in which not they alone but Christian Europe was engaged. To speak of Beauclerk as having shown ingratitude to his archbishop because he did not acknowledge a personal obligation by the surrender of a constitutional prerogative of his Crown is to misunderstand the two men and the issue before them. The debate was one on State policy. Nor was this the method of settlement which Anselm desired. His desire was that the relation of primate to king, of Church to State should be put upon a definite legal basis which would free the Church from the arbitrary encroachments or the embarrassing aid of any king. Gently but patiently he pursued that end. The scope of the question grew upon him, till he is found writing to the new king of Jerusalem that there was nothing God so loved on earth as the liberty of His Church. His past seven years of work in England had convinced him of the hopelessness of any good relations between king and archbishop, so long as everything depended on the will of an individual. He asked therefore for no personal consideration but the dispassionate settlement of a question of constitutional law. And Henry so treated it. He did not always maintain his self-control, nor did he always display the same Christian courtesy which Anselm showed to him, but it would be the heaviest indictment one could lay against the Church in any period, that Churchmen were inferior to laymen in methods of controversy.

In the end of the year the envoys arrived with Paschal's reply. Behind its phrases of goodwill to the king and its lengthy citations from Holy Scripture and from the past contendings of emperors and bishops rested the fact that on one point the popes refused to yield. On investiture Rome did not mean to give way : on homage the letter discreetly said nothing. The pope was further careful to avoid the immediate question as to how king and archbishop in England were to act towards each other. Paschal had no desire to quarrel with Henry, he could not forego the support of England's allegiance, even the material support of Peter's pence. Henry was as little inclined to break with Rome, since an open breach would have made more difficult his present difficult situation. Both sides therefore confined themselves to generalities.

Anselm was summoned to the court, and on his arrival was asked what he meant to do. He replied by an appeal to the canons of the councils in which he had taken part. The pope's letter had confirmed his opinion as to their meaning. Were he to disobey those decisions, he would in that very act be rendering himself excommunicate ; and he did not mean to cut himself off from the Church. "I have nothing to do with those questions," the king answered ; "what I have to do with is that I will not lose the customs of my predecessors, nor tolerate within this realm anyone who is not man of mine." "I understand the issue," replied the archbishop. " But I do not mean to leave the realm. I shall go down to my church and diocese and while doing my duty there shall leave you to determine whether you mean to do violence to me or mine." The discussion was evidently half-hearted. Each party was too clear-sighted not to see the hopeless opposition between their rival principles. Neither was yet prepared to yield anything to the other, but both were unwilling to take action by prosecution or excommunication. Anselm wished, if a rupture did take place, to throw the onus of attack on the king, and the king realised the disadvantage his cause would suffer if he openly attacked a man whom he and his whole kingdom held in high esteem.

For a time a breach seemed imminent; but Henry was too prudent to have two troubles on his hands at once, and at this time the Earl of Shrewsbury was suspected of fomenting disturbances in the West of England. There were the usual messages between court and prelate, blustering on the one side, calmly self-restrained on the other. There were the usual lengthy diplomatic interlocutors which led to nothing. But when it became evident that war could not be avoided in the West the king proposed the despatch of another embassy, more honourable and better instructed, to Rome. Anselm consented: two monks, Baldwin and Alexander, from the Christ Church convent were sent to represent the archbishop, while Henry was represented by Gerard, archbishop of York, Herbert, bishop of Norwich, and Robert, bishop of Chester.

The king was no sooner free from the ecclesiastical difficulty than he turned to crush Robert of Belesme, and in one swift campaign drove the earl into exile, and proved to England once for all that it had found its master. Not without reason did Orderic with a reminiscence of classical erudition introduce the genius of England as addressing Henry after his victory. "Rejoice, O king, and render thanks to God the Lord for this, that thou hast now begun to be a free king, since thou hast overthrown Robert of Belesme and driven him beyond thy realm." The English people whom Henry had trusted had not failed him in two issues: henceforth his crown was secure.

At a great council held in London 1102 the question of the Church came to be considered. The messengers had returned from Rome, and the king demanded that Anselm should now do him right in the debate between them. The archbishop claimed that the letter which the envoys had brought back to the king be read, and showed to all a letter from Paschal which justified him in the attitude he had assumed. Henry however refused to make public the letter he had received. When its contents did come to be known the reason for concealing them was obvious, for in it Paschal unhesitatingly refused to permit the king liberty in the investiture of bishops, and holding to the usual fiction that the royal advisers were responsible for the claim, urged him to reject the advice of men who were leading him astray. That of course left the door open for further negotiations and saved the pope the unwelcome task of breaking with the king. Instead however of allowing this letter to be read, Henry appealed to his messengers. The three bishops brought a strange tale.

They declared that in a private interview Paschal had traversed all his previous utterances, and had declared himself content that Henry should invest with staff and ring, so long as he was heedful to promote "religious persons" to the bishoprics. As an explanation of the singular fact that a decision of this gravity was conveyed by word of mouth, the bishops stated that Paschal feared to commit the resolution to writing lest the other kings of Europe hearing of the privilege granted to England should claim the same. They further declared on the same authority that the archbishop was ordered to accept their statement as his commission for consecrating the bishops whom Henry chose to invest.

Naturally Anselm's envoys protested. They appealed to the official letter which the archbishop had received, demanded that the letter to Henry should be produced, and hinted at faithlessness on the part of the bishops. Recrimination between the parties grew hot. The king's party insolently refused in connection with a high affair of State to accept the evidence of monks, men who had abjured all interest in mere mundane matters. But, objected Baldwin, this is no mere affair of State, it is an affair of the most directly religious moment. No matter, was the answer, we know you to be both wise and zealous; but you have no right to expect that the testimony of a few monks should outweigh the testimony of high-placed and honourable Churchmen like the bishops. That may be so, retorted the monk, but what of the letters? Pshaw, letters are after all no more than pieces of sheepskin with a lump of lead hung to them. We count them of little moment against the evidence of an archbishop.

What? cried the scandalised monk. The Gospels are mere sheepskins. Will you say the same about them?

Opinion on the veracity of the bishops will always vary, since the evidence is not sufficient to decide the matter with finality. It is not very credible that the pope gave a definite instruction in a letter and contradicted it in a verbal message. On the other hand it is equally difficult of belief that three Churchmen (to credit them with no higher motive) were so foolish as to proffer that plain statement without some support for it. They had enough knowledge of public affairs to know that Anselm would never accept so far-reaching a decision without inquiry into the reason why it conflicted with his instructions. Had they invented the whole story, they must have known that its falsity was sure to be revealed. The probability is—and Paschal's silence about homage in the letters strengthens it— that the pope in a private interview, when Anselm's messengers were absent, expressed himself in terms which were less rigorous than those of his letters. The Roman court always found Anselm too uncompromising to make a facile negotiator. Paschal may have expressed that, and the bishops, wishing to please their king and not sharing their primate's position in the whole matter, may have exaggerated every hint of a possible relaxation. Consciously or unconsciously they heightened all the colours in their report, made definite what the pope had left vague, and turned into a public declaration what was meant as a private hint to the king's ear in order to soften the severe *non possumus* attitude of the letters.

The statement by the bishops, whether true or false, gained the king what he most desired, time. It was necessary to send a new embassy to Rome and request fresh instructions. Anselm's letter had a little more insistence in its tone. "I have heard in the council of Rome my lord Urban of venerable memory excommunicate kings and laity who should grant investitures and intromit with Church property, and those who accepted such investiture or did homage in such circumstances, and those who consecrate ecclesiastics who receive such investiture. Let your holiness then be pleased to remove this excommunication from England, that I may remain there without peril to my own soul, or make me know that you intend to maintain it at all hazards, or, if it please your prudence to make certain reserves, be pleased to indicate them to me in a sure way. I ask further to be determined by an order on your side concerning what I ought to do with regard to those who during this truce may receive investiture and with regard to those who consecrate them." Anselm had learned at Rome some of the difficulties which crowded round the supreme see. He had no wish to embarrass the pope by taking precipitate action on his own authority. Rather did he put himself unreservedly in Paschal's hands, and recognise that if the Church were to act powerfully in this matter it must act unitedly. The rôle suited the temper of the archbishop, who was ever stronger in passive resistance than in initiative.

The last sentence of the letter refers to the agreement according to which Henry was to be at liberty to invest new bishops, while Anselm, though not required to consecrate them, was not to refuse communion with them. The king proceeded in accordance with the agreement to appoint Roger a court chancellor

to the see of Salisbury, and another Roger the royal
larderer to that of Hereford.   One of these men had
won the king's high approval, because, on a morning
when Henry attended Mass before going to hunt, he
had shown an extraordinary power of racing through
the divine service.   That was Henry's idea of what
qualified the "religious persons" whom according to
the episcopal messengers he was empowered to invest
with the charge of men's souls.   Practically Anselm
was fighting for the right on the part of the Church to
refuse nominees of such a type.   When Henry ignoring
the terms of their truce required the archbishop to
consecrate these two, he firmly refused.   The king had
already appointed William Giffard to be bishop of
Winchester, and, since he was worthy of the office and
had not accepted investiture from the king, Anselm
was willing to consecrate Giffard.   But this Henry
refused to allow and demanded that the archbishop
must consecrate all three or none.   The motive was
obvious, too obvious to deceive any man of intelligence.
During the delay larderer Roger died, vainly begging
the primate to grant him the grace of consecration
even on his deathbed.   The archbishop only smiled at
a petition the pathetic illogicality of which it was not
in his nature to understand.

Henry appointed Reinhelm one of the queen's household to the vacant see, and, when Anselm again refused
to consecrate, ordered the Archbishop of York to carry
out the rite.   It was a distinct breach of agreement
and a contemptible move.   Yet Gerard of York, jealous
of the prerogatives of Canterbury and perhaps hoping
to make favour at the court for life, was prepared to
obey.   But suddenly men learned to their surprise that

Reinhelm, courtier though he was, had sent back staff and ring to the king with the declaration that he counted a consecration on these terms no blessing but a curse. A greater surprise however was in store. The bishops were assembled in the church in London for the consecration of Roger and Giffard, when the latter also rebelled. Pressure of the coarse kind which the age understood was brought to bear on him, but persuasion and threats were alike useless. He knew from what Reinhelm had suffered all that was in store for him, but he rejected consecration on these terms.

Beauclerk drove the rebels from the court and stripped them of their property. But the event was significant, and he was shrewd enough to recognise that he had gone too far. A new sense of their responsibility was growing among the higher clergy in England. Anselm's steady protest had not been wholly wasted. The humiliation of a position which put the Church's leaders at the mercy of one man was penetrating even into courtiers. When it penetrated the seared conscience of a courtier, it could no longer be ignored. Unintentionally the king aided the movement; he allowed a synod of the English clergy to be summoned at Westminster on September 29 1102. No synod had met in the kingdom for twenty-six years. The decisions of the council are interesting in the light they cast on the social condition of England, and are especially interesting since they show the aims which earnest Churchmen set before them. Side by side is found the condemnation of those who traffic in "men like brute beasts," and of those who traffic in ecclesiastical offices, of the sons of priests who inherit their fathers' churches and of the abbots who dub men knights, of the clergy who refuse to put away their wives and of the laity who persist in wearing long hair. More significant to Beauclerk in his struggle with Anselm was the fact that six abbots were deposed for simony and three for causes of a similar character. That was a direct challenge to the court, for the men had been appointed by the king and the first act of a synod was to condemn them. No sooner was the Church allowed a voice in its corporate capacity than it used its new-found liberty. The Stuarts were wise when they forbade General Assemblies of the Kirk. Men who had been afraid to utter a protest when they stood alone were not afraid to utter it in their joint capacity, especially since their archbishop and not they would bear the brunt of the king's anger. Even the fact that the men had met and realised their common mission as the leaders of the Church within England helped to spread the new spirit.

Beauclerk felt the ground slipping away beneath him, and knew that the cause of all was Anselm. He made one last effort to treat with his primate apart from Rome. Appearing suddenly in Canterbury he attempted to persuade Anselm to yield, but was met by the reply that the letters from Rome which the king himself had desired were on their way. Beauclerk grew angry. The blood of the Conqueror was in his veins, and he could ill brook any restraint. Besides he may have honestly resented the hard measure which was meted out to him. He had yielded everything which the Church vainly demanded during the reign of his brother, had surrendered all the property of the sees, had refused to interfere with the Church's management of its property, had permitted free intercourse

to be restored with Rome and had recently suffered a
synod to meet within his realm.   His only reward for
all this consideration was that the Church treated him
worse than it had treated Rufus, that mocker at all
religion and spoiler of the Church.

Whether the king fairly lost his self-control for
a time, or, not knowing the man with whom he had
to deal, tried to terrify Anselm into submission the
royal attitude became very menacing.   Men dreaded
a return to the old violent measures of Rufus.   Prayers
were offered in many places for the safety of the
archbishop.    But, when the letters arrived from
Rome, the king suddenly changed his tone.    He
refused to publish the letter which the pope had
communicated to him; but from the letter which was
sent to Anselm there can be no doubt as to its tenor.
It became evident to the king that he could only
gain his end by temporising or by a final rupture
with Rome.   Since from motives of religion or policy
he was not prepared to break with Rome, he chose
to temporise; and he proposed that Anselm should
himself go to Rome and lay the whole position of
affairs before Paschal.   By this means Henry hoped
at least to free himself of the man who was the
nerve of the entire movement.

After some hesitation the archbishop consented.
He too had received a letter from the pope, but
he refused to open it because, if it were found un-
sealed, his enemies were not incapable of declaring
that he had falsified the contents.   A further reason,
however, which made him willing to leave the country
and unwilling to open the letter until he was beyond
England, was that he had good cause to suspect its

contents. He felt sure it contained an intimation
that Paschal had already excommunicated the bishops
who had brought the false report from Rome, and
counted it possible that it notified the excommunication of the king. He was accordingly afraid lest
he should run the risk of his soul's hurt, were he to
continue in association with men who were under
the ban of the Church. The fact, it may be added,
that Anselm counted this likely is a clear proof
of what in his opinion the pope ought to do. He
expected the pope to take the initiative. Since the
disobedience had been against the canons of a council
of the whole Church, it was for the official head
of the Church to visit that disobedience with the
Church's censure. Anselm was prepared to support
such action.

But the archbishop only consented to go to Rome,
if that was the desire of the nation. At the Easter
court which met in Winchester 1103 the request
was made by the entire council. Anselm made no
delay but crossed at once to Le Bec. There on
opening his letter from the pope he found his ex-
pectations partly fulfilled. The pope had excommunicated not only the bishops who brought the
false report, but all who relying on their statement
had accepted investiture at the king's hands, because
even the prophet whom a prophet had deceived did
not escape death. This last journey to Rome on
which Anselm set out was very different from that
which he made under Rufus. He departed in all
honour and outward respect. Henry had no desire
to resort to extreme measures. The prelate had
offered a gentle but invincible opposition. Evidently

then a conflict with him meant embarrassment but no danger. Henry need not fear that his archbishop would put him under the ban. Yet it was better for Henry's plans that Anselm should be quietly removed out of the way, for the synod had shown how capable he was of inspiring the Church with a new spirit of resistance. It is further possible that the king counted on the fact that the old man would be averse to prolonging the struggle and might do his best toward bringing the Roman court to a more practicable temper in order to secure peace. If that was his hope, the result deceived it, for his gentle opponent by very meekness stiffened the resistance of Rome.

# CHAPTER XII

## THE CONCORDAT

THERE followed a series of negotiations which are somewhat tedious to trace in detail. On the one side was the cautious and unscrupulous Henry, who was seeking to maintain unimpaired all the privileges of the Crown, but who was unwilling to involve himself in an open quarrel with the Church. Throughout he played the game of delay, because the archbishop was already an old man worn with fasting, and his successor might prove more pliable. On the other side was the court of Rome, which had begun to see that a compromise was inevitable and was therefore too cautious to commit itself to an extreme position which would give that compromise the appearance of a surrender. And between these was Anselm, uncompromisingly holding to the orders he had received from Church councils, and by his mild tenacity shaming the pope into at least an appearance of firmness.

When Anselm landed at Wissant, he found himself at once among friends, all of whom were eager to offer him hospitality. But no place was so grateful to him as the old nest at Le Bec, and no society so congenial as that of fellow-monks: at Le Bec he accordingly lingered about three months. The summer of this year was peculiarly sultry, and all who loved him urged him not to venture into the heats of Italy till the cooler season. Even Henry wrote to suggest that his archbishop should not weary himself by a difficult journey, but be content with sending an envoy to transact the negotiations at Rome. It may be legitimate to suspect that the new solicitude was only partly due to personal regard, and that the king desired to keep his archbishop away from both Rome and England. The letter however did not reach the exile till he was already at Maurienne on his southward road; and, contenting himself with a courteous reply, he pressed on.

At Rome he was received with all honour, and lodged in the rooms at the Vatican which had been Urban's gift to the "pope of the second world." There too William of Warelwast soon appeared, diligent as ever about the business of his new master, skilful as ever in the manipulation of strings which his opponent disdained to touch. The cause came to be heard before the Curia. Warelwast pleaded strongly the peculiar circumstances in which the King of England was placed, and urged the evil influence it would produce on his policy if Rome branded with its disapproval a ruler of his character, after the ungodly Rufus had escaped all censure. His appeal, supported by means of persuasion more powerful than words, produced some effect, for signs of agreement were visible among his auditors. In an unguarded moment the envoy clinched the situation with great brusqueness. "Let what will be said on this side or on that, all men may take it as certain

that, not even to save his crown, will King Henry
surrender his rights of investiture." But the pope
was not to be browbeaten in this fashion before his
own court. "As God is my witness," was Paschal's
retort, "not to save his head will the pope suffer
the king to claim with impunity control over the
churches."

These were "prave orts." It remained to be
seen what Paschal meant to do. A new papal letter
was prepared for England. It abounded in compli-
ments and congratulations to the king over the birth
of his firstborn son, it granted Henry the free
exercise of certain unknown privileges which his
father had enjoyed, but it maintained the principle
of the Church's right to investiture, and pronounced
excommunicate all who had received or should accept
investiture at the king's hands. Yet the letter carefully refrained from touching the king, the head
and front of the offence. When the letter arrived
in England, Henry drew from it the conclusion that,
if Paschal had been free to act after his own wishes,
he would have found some excuse for permitting the
king to evade obedience to the canons. He diligently
represented both to his council and to his people
that Anselm was finally responsible for this severity.
And certainly the letter leaves that impression. The
pope, with the instinct for evading responsibility
and direct action which belongs to weak men, persisted in laying the blame for Henry's action on the
counsellors who had given him bad advice, and suggested that his own severity of tone was due to the
necessity of his position. One clause in the letter
runs, "Ask thyself whether it be to thy credit or

discredit that a bishop like Anselm whom all the world honours must remain without the country because of thine action." The words have little meaning, unless Warelwast had informed the pope how Henry, in the event of Rome refusing to yield, had determined to treat his archbishop; and the fact that Rome with this knowledge abstained from any stronger measures was a sufficient hint that Henry was free to act toward Anselm as he pleased. In one thing the letter succeeded; it kept the door open for negotiations between Rome and England.

There was nothing further for Anselm to do in Rome. He quitted the city towards the end of November, and was escorted across the dangerous district of the Apennines by a guard from the famous Countess Matilda. Like him she was growing old, and perhaps a little weary of a life which had been one of continual struggle. She consulted the archbishop as to whether she might not now enter religion and, leaving the field where she had so long fought the battles of Holy Church, devote the evening of her days to prayer for her own soul. In his letter of thanks for her protection Anselm dissuaded her from the step. She could serve God and the Church better in the estate in which she was. The utmost he allowed was that she should keep a nun's dress beside her, and assume it during her last hours. God, who knew her heart's desire and who had sent the hindering duties, would take the will for the deed. Yet Anselm had once and again refused to allow that a man's family relations were sufficient cause to prevent him from undertaking monastic vows. A narrow construction of religious duty was the weak-

ness of monasticism, and even this beautiful spirit
did not escape its influence.

At Piacenza the unwearied Warelwast overtook the
travellers.   When the two parties separated in Rome,
he had expressed the intention of making a pilgrimage
to the tomb of St. Nicholas at Bari.   The monks drily
complimented him on the rapid travelling which had
made it possible for him to fulfil his vow and yet
overtake them on the road.   They suspected that St.
Nicholas did not receive all Warelwast's votive offer-
ings.   Together the two companies crossed the Alps,
but, before they reached Lyons where Anselm pur-
posed to pass the Christmas season, the envoy delivered
himself of what was practically an ultimatum.   " I
withheld from you at Rome the final commission of my
king, because I anticipated that our business there
would receive a different issue; but I must tell it you
now.   If you mean to come back to England and be to
him what former archbishops were to former kings,
he will hail your coming."   " Have you," answered
the archbishop, " anything further to add ? "   " I am
speaking to a man of understanding," was the reply.
" And I understand," Anselm answered.   There was no
need for further words.   The Christmas season was to
begin a new period of exile.

Anselm's position was not an easy one.   The action
which Rome had seen fit to take thrust him into a very
difficult situation.   He could not on the ground of the
investiture question take open action against Henry.
The king's disobedience was against no law of the
primate's creation : it was against the law of the whole
Church.   It was for the earthly head of the Church to
condone or to condemn that contumacy.   Since Rome

had practically condoned the offence by refraining from excommunication of the king, it would have been an arrogating of powers which he had no right to claim and a tacit condemnation of the action of Rome, had the archbishop proceeded to any overt act against the king. On the other hand Rome's action made it impossible for him to return to England, for the pope, while hesitating to strike the chief offender, had laid under the ban all bishops who accepted investiture from the king. If then Anselm returned to England, he could not exercise his office and avoid communion with these men. Yet if he held relations with them he brought the guilt of intercommunion with anathematised persons on himself and belittled in men's eyes the sentence of excommunication under which they lay. The only means of avoiding such intercourse was to live in practical retirement in some monastery or manor of his diocese. He judged it better to find his place of retirement in Lyons. To remain at Lyons implied an equal inactivity so far as the archiepiscopal duties were concerned, and presented a clearer, more intelligible protest.

Yet the fact that he elected to remain at Lyons exposed Anselm to an inevitable misconstruction. What most men in England saw was that their new king was prepared to treat the Church with a respect which it had never received from Rufus, but that the leader of the Church refused their king what he had granted without hesitation to Rufus. Beauclerk was careful to represent matters from this point of view, and to maintain a cautious respect for the rights of the Church. He whispered that this was not the primate England needed, this scholar and saint, who was more

15

monk than archbishop, and who preferred to remain in an idle peace at Lyons rather than undertake the charge of his diocese at home.

Anselm's letters during the year and a half he spent in Lyons take a new edge of directness, as he insists on the principles involved in his act. "It appears," so he wrote to the prior of Christ Church, "as though I were shunning my duty without cause. . . . It is not that I shun duty, but that I cannot fulfil my duty where and as I ought. Men there are, and you know their names, with whom I cannot communicate without peril to my own soul. Yet if I entered into close relations with the king, I could not avoid communion with them. What should I do for instance were I to go to court in order to crown the king and say mass, while these men stood beside me? I cannot expel them from the chapel-royal; I dare not pray with them; I must not withhold my customary duty from the king, since he has a right to expect it and the pope has enjoined it." The hopeless dilemma into which the papal action had thrust him was manifest, but he left others to draw the conclusion. With entire loyalty he nowhere permitted himself a word of complaint against the court whose hesitation was exposing him to cruel misconstruction. And he closed his letter with a vigorous sentence: "One thing I wish you to know: it is my resolution with God's help to make myself no man's vassal and to swear fealty to no man."

It was on this resolution, its novelty and its danger, that the king and his counsellors continually fastened. And the main strength of the king's position was that he could appeal to Lanfranc's attitude toward the same demand. No previous archbishop of England had hesi-

tated to swear fealty: why should this one refuse?
What right had Anselm to rob his lord of the honour
which was the royal due from every subject in
England? What right had the bishops to make themselves different from all other men in the realm?
Anselm felt the difficulty, as a letter to the king shows.
"Your Majesty deigns to send me the assurance of
your friendship, and to add that there is none whom
you would more willingly receive within your kingdom
than myself, if I would but consent to be with you
on the same terms as Lanfranc was with your father.
For your goodwill I thank you, but with reference to
the other matter I reply that neither in baptism nor at
my ordination did I pledge myself to observe the law
or custom of your father or of Lanfranc, but the law of
God and the law imposed on me by my orders."

On this again his opponents fastened; the king especially resented it as a slight on his father's memory,
since he interpreted it to imply a censure alike on
Lanfranc and on the Conqueror. Did Anselm mean
to suggest that his predecessor had not promised to
observe the law of God and the law of his orders?
Was this archbishop the first who understood the
sacredness of his office? The misrepresentation stung
the archbishop who had no thought of claiming for
himself a superior righteousness. He wrote to Queen
Matilda: "I have said nothing against the king's
father and Archbishop Lanfranc, men of great and
venerable name" (in the extract from the letter to the
king quoted above). "As to the demand urged on me
and supported by their action I cannot perform it
because of what I heard with my own ears at Rome."
But how keenly he felt the allegation is specially

apparent in a letter to his old friend Gondulf of Rochester. "Some meddlesome mischief-maker out of the villainy of his own heart has explained my letter to the king as though I professed ever to have kept the law of God, and as though I slandered the king's father and Lanfranc as men who neglected that law. The men who say such things have either a narrow or a malicious mind. For in their time these men, great and venerable as they were, did what in my time I cannot without peril to my own soul."

More than a year passed, letters and messengers came and went across the Channel. But meantime Henry took a false step. After Warelwast's return the king proceeded to lay hands on the property of the see of Canterbury. The confiscation was not so complete nor so insolently effected as under Rufus. Henry forwarded part of the revenue to its rightful owner with a courteous message that it was by no wish of his the archbishop was not in peaceful possession of the whole. And no royal officers but two men of the archbishop were appointed commissioners to take charge of the confiscated estates and remit the money to the fisc. None the less was it from the royal point of view a false step. It gave Anselm the opportunity of independent action, since the king by his act had come into conflict, not with the law of the universal Church, but with the special rights of the see of Canterbury. Its archbishop could now vindicate those rights by his own authority without waiting for Rome.

There seemed however a last hope of intervention from Rome on the larger question. During the summer of 1104 Henry had sent another embassy to Paschal. A council was to be held at Rome, and the position of affairs in England was to come before it. From Lyons the trusty Baldwin was despatched to represent the archbishop's position, and Anselm wrote an urgent letter to his old friend John of Telese, now bishop of Tusculum, in which he besought him to take heed that no harm was done at the council to the authority of the holy see. Other supporters, among them the Countess Matilda, brought strong pressure to bear on Paschal in the interest of Anselm. At last men hoped for definite and final action against Henry, but Paschal in the Lenten Council of 1105 confined himself to the excommunication of the king's counsellors, especially of Robert of Meulan, who was regarded as his chief adviser in his ecclesiastical action. The pope pronounced it impossible to proceed against the king, because the latter had promised to send further envoys after Easter.

This decision only added to the number of those with whom Anselm, if he returned to England, could hold no communion, and made his return more difficult than ever. Anselm saw that it was idle to expect further help from Rome, and reluctantly resolved to act independently against the king on the ground of his confiscation of the Canterbury revenues. At this time Henry was in Normandy. The uneasy peace between the brothers had come to its inevitable end, as all men except the unready Robert had foreseen, and the younger brother had crossed the Channel and begun war.

Anselm left Lyons and proceeded north into Champagne. Hearing that Countess Adela, the daughter of the Conqueror, was dangerously ill at Blois, he turned aside to visit her there. He found her convalescent, and did not conceal that the object of his journey was to excommunicate her brother. The countess was deeply moved by the news, and persuaded the archbishop to return to Chartres while she made the attempt to persuade Henry and avoid an open rupture. Henry was amenable to reason. His position in Normandy and his aims there made it exceedingly desirable that he should not be under the ban of the Church. The fact that Philip of France had been compelled only a year before to humble himself and sue for peace with the Church proved how much power an excommunication exercised over men's minds. These things may have had more influence over the wily king than even the persuasions of his sister.

A meeting was accordingly arranged between the king and his archbishop at Laigle between Séez and Mortagne on July 22. So far as concerned their personal quarrel, Henry frankly acknowledged the wrong he had done in laying hands on the property of the see, and undertook to restore not only the property but even the revenues which he had already appropriated. He refused however to abandon the Churchmen who had given him their support, and required the primate not to decline intercommunion with such as had accepted bishoprics at the royal hands. In connection with the larger question between Church and State Henry proposed one of those compromises which seem so impossible in the heat of the struggle and so obvious when the heat has cooled. The king surrendered the right of investiture : staff and ring, the symbols of spiritual authority, were to be delivered into the hands of the bishop by the Church, and thus the right of the Church as the only source of spiritual authority was openly recognised. But the

Church on its part was to pay homage: a bishop like every other subject was to acknowledge his fealty to the king, and pledge in customary form his loyal service to the State.

The Concordat must be referred to the pope. Only Paschal could finally ratify it, and only Paschal could free from the Church's ban the men in England whom he had laid under excommunication, and authorise the archbishop to hold communion with them. Until a reply returned from Rome, Anselm remained in Normandy, he refused to enter England until his position and power there were made perfectly clear. But the archbishop had secret scruples about consenting to return, even if Rome, as he foresaw, consented to accept the Concordat. He had become in this matter *papa papalior*. The pope would doubtless allow the prelate to consecrate a bishop, even if that bishop had paid homage to the king. But what if a bishop refused to pay homage? Must the archbishop refuse him consecration until he had satisfied the royal demands, and so use his authority either to compel a scrupulous conscience into an act which several councils had declared to merit excommunication, or to drive out of the Church its best men?

While the embassy was on its way to Rome, Anselm consulted his old friend Hugh of Lyons on the subject. "The whole difficulty between the king and me seems to be that, whilst allowing himself, as I hope, to submit to the papal decisions on investitures of churches, he is not yet disposed to surrender the homages of prelates and is resorting to the holy see in hope of getting leave to do as he wishes in this particular. Should he succeed however I do not know how to act, if any man of religion were to refuse upon election to become the king's man for any bishopric or abbacy. It seems a hard thing to require such a candidate on his obedience to do this, and yet if I do not I shall evidently be paving the way for the unworthy entrance into those dignities of such as not being men of religion may have no scruple on the subject." The Archbishop of Lyons had not always found himself in perfect agreement with Rome, but in this case he strongly advised his brother to give way. "I beg and advise you, for I write in the double capacity of suppliant and coun- sellor, to yield an unaffected submission to the pope's orders, so that you may not seem to set more store by your own opinion than by his authority, and thus incur the reproach of resisting not only the temporal and royal authority but the ecclesiastical and priestly. And yet unhappy man that I am," he adds in a sentence which shows as clearly the tender relations between the two men as the significance which he attached to papal censure, "in this I become the author and instigator of my own loss, since I strive to remove one who after God is my only comfort and my only joy, the life of my soul, from the sight of those eyes which I now seem to employ uselessly, since that which they were wont to enjoy, namely, the sight of my well-beloved friend, it will not be granted them to see and even to hope ever to see again. Yet far be it from me that for my own temporary advantage I should envy the general salvation of so many souls; verily I will not seek my own things, but the things of Jesus Christ."

The letter from the pope arrived in the spring of 1106, and as Anselm had foreseen accepted practically the terms of Henry's Concordat, while it sought to safeguard the principle. Homage was allowed, and the prelate was authorised to consecrate bishops who had paid it; but care was taken that this was only a permission in present circumstances, and the hope was expressed that Anselm might be able through his personal influence to persuade the king into the surrender of this point also. Anselm was further empowered to grant absolution to all the excommunicated bishops in England, even to those who had brought the false report back from Rome.

Not yet however was the archbishop free to return to his duty in England. Both before the embassy was sent to Rome and after the letter arrived there were long delays. Henry was busy with his war against Normandy, and caught at every excuse which could postpone the final settlement. While Anselm was involved in negotiations, he was at least powerless to interfere with the king's other schemes. Now it was the stormy weather which prevented his envoys from crossing the Channel. Again he wrote to say that he had learned there were two popes fighting with each other in Rome, and to suggest that it were better to wait and see which of them was to come out conqueror. When the papal letter had made it clear that Rome was not impracticable on the question, the king became more anxious to have his venerable prelate back to England. But now sickness fell on Anselm. The end was beginning to threaten after his many toils and self-imposed privations. At Le Bec he was brought so near to death that the abbots of the neighbourhood assembled for the last rites. The king hastened to the monastery and was now profuse in the evidences of an

unfeigned affection when it could no longer be misunderstood. The two men, so unlike in many things,
so like in many others, reached some recognition each
of the other's position before they separated, the archbishop to return to his duty at Canterbury, the king
to prosecute the war in Normandy.

At last Anselm, with every question determined so
far as Henry and himself were concerned, crossed the
Channel and was received with the utmost enthusiasm
at Dover in September 1106. But England was not
an absolute monarchy; that the powers of the Crown
were not exactly defined did not mean that the English
people had no voice. The question which had been
so long and variously debated between Henry and
Anselm was a constitutional question, involving an
arrangement which deeply modified the powers and
the rights of the Crown in England. Even when king
and archbishop had seen their way to a settlement,
the matter must come before the council of the realm.
Until however the war in Normandy was at an end,
nothing could be done towards a final settlement.

In the end of September Henry was able to write to
the archbishop and announce the victory of Tinchebray
which made Normandy his own. It is one out of many
illustrations which prove the strange confusion of men's
moral judgments in the Middle Age to read how the
victory was regarded by Eadmer and by many of the
monastic party. Henry had ventured upon a wholly
unjust war against his brother Robert. The only
justification which could be found for it was mere
revenge for Robert's earlier attack on England, a plea
which ought to have formed an additional condemnation of the war in the judgment of Churchmen. Henry

had taken his brother prisoner, he was to keep him for many years in a dungeon and finally, with no one venturing a protest against the deed, was to put out his eyes. Yet many of the party who were the strongest supporters of ecclesiastical reform counted it certain that Tinchebray was a crowning mercy which God had seen fit to grant their king because of the peace he had patched up with his archbishop. So easy is it to tithe mint and to pass over justice.

The Concordat between the Church and the State came for final determination before a great council held at London in August 1107, and there the question was again debated keenly. It is a mistake to imagine that the unwillingness to surrender to the demands of the Church arose merely from the personal pride and ambition of Norman kings. Often they merely represented the opinions of their counsellors, sometimes they were clearer of vision on the question than these. Men in England were proud of their kingdom, its liberties and its privileges, and were not inclined to suffer the decisions of an Italian bishop to rob the Crown of its dignity and above all of its independence. A passage from one of Beauclerk's letters to a pope after Anselm's death proves how difficult the king often found his situation between two contending forces. " There is no end, as there is no measure, to their (the barons' and vassals') taunts and gibes. They tell me that, thanks to my remissness and want of zeal in asserting them, I am suffering the old prestige and the rights hitherto kept inviolate of my kingdom to be filched away from me." But at this particular council Henry had given his word, and he held stoutly to the arrangement he had made.

It might have been possible for him, now that Normandy was in his power and all his dominions loyally supported him, now that the Church's censure was less to be dreaded, to have resiled from his agreement and to have thrown the blame of the rupture on the fact that he could not persuade his barons. But the character of Anselm had won the entire respect of his king, and had summoned into evidence all the best elements in his nature. He honoured the archbishop, now one of the best known men in Europe, with such honour as it was in him to pay. He recognised that the presence of such a man was an honour to his kingdom and a strength to his throne. If Anselm would only consent to come on certain terms, Henry after due consideration of the terms was prepared to grant them. By the firmness of the king and the archbishop the matter was finally arranged, and the Concordat of Laigle was accepted as the rule to govern Church and State in their mutual relations within England. The peace was publicly manifested in the solemn act of August 11 1107, when Anselm consecrated five bishops to vacant sees in England. One of them, it is interesting to note, was his indefatigable opponent William of Warelwast.

# CHAPTER XIII

## Conclusion

ANSELM'S battles with the State were now at an end,
but he had no long time to reap the fruits of victory.
The keen sword was wearing through its scabbard,
and already the hand of death was on him. Yet
it was not granted him to close his life in peace; he
must struggle against the spirit of rebellion which had
made its way among his clergy.

He had the satisfaction at Whitsuntide 1108 of
presiding over a great council of clergy and laity which
came together to consider the condition of the Church
in England. His struggle with the State had always
had as its most powerful motive to win for the Church
the opportunity to do her distinctive work within the
kingdom. Now, when the opportunity was won, the
Church must be instant to use it. The first peace with
Henry had been employed to convene one council; no
sooner was the Concordat arranged than a second was
summoned. The chief question which engaged the
attention of the assembled Churchmen was the condition of the parochial clergy. In accordance with the
monkish ideals which the Benedictine revival had
brought with it stringent regulations were passed to en-
force celibacy on the whole body of the secular clergy.

On that subject England had remained saner than the Continent, but now the new ideas had their way.

Anselm had the further satisfaction of using the high esteem in which he was held by the king in order to check the licence of the court. Whenever the court journeyed through England, it had been in the habit of billeting itself on the village where it chose to pass the night and of living at free cost on the villagers. Like other plagues the members of the court destroyed more than they used. With the insolence which easily creeps on the courtier in his behaviour toward the bucolic, with the added insolence which arose from the courtier being a Norman and the rustic a Saxon, the destruction became wanton. Men saw their homes practically pillaged, the food which their visitors could not consume tossed carelessly to the dogs or the fire, the surplus of their wine used to wash the feet of horses; men experienced those worse outrages which receive no forgiveness. So notorious had the conduct of the court grown, that, when the news reached a village of a probable visit from their king, the inhabitants often left their homes *en masse*, not to return till the locusts had departed. The archbishop showed a true sense that he was father in God to all his flock and set over them to be the reconciler of the divided interests and races in England. At his earnest representation Henry sternly put down the worst of these abuses.

Discipline within the Church itself had not escaped scathless from the long absences of its primate. Bishops had learned the dangerous habit of liberty and of defiance to constituted authority. The Archbishop of York had always been jealous of the primacy of Canterbury, but had had little need to show resentment since the superior was so rarely present to exert his authority. No sooner however was Anselm fairly installed, and the theory threatened to become a practical reality, than York rebelled. Gerard was dead, and a successor elected in his place. He must according to rule appear in Canterbury for consecration and promise obedience to his superior. Flambard after many strange experiences had reappeared as bishop of Durham. It may have been at his instigation that the archbishop-elect delayed to present himself in Canterbury, wrote direct to Rome for the grant of his pallium, and without having been consecrated himself prepared to consecrate a bishop for St. Andrews. Anselm sent a strong remonstrance and warned his brother-archbishop that, if the canonical months elapsed without his having sought consecration from his primate, his election might be voided. At the same time he wrote to represent the position of affairs at Rome, and asked that the pallium, if forwarded at all, should be forwarded to Canterbury, whence it could be transmitted to York when Thomas had tendered his submission. The archbishop-elect tried every means of evasion and delay. He represented the poverty of his see and his own lack of money as the excuse for his failure to proceed southward, but betrayed clearly that he hoped to postpone the whole question until the age and sickness of the primate had made the see of Canterbury vacant. But Anselm was not to be moved. The due subordination of office within the Church was to him an axiom in its efficient government, whether or not the presence of the hierarchy were essential to the Church's existence as the Church of Christ. He sent a sharp warning to Rome (for he knew his Rome) that, if there were any trifling with his position in the matter, he would refuse to remain in England. And one of his last letters was an equally sharp and curt epistle to Thomas of York, in which it was intimated that, unless his submission were proffered within a certain period, interdict would be pronounced.

Interdict however was never to be pronounced by Anselm. The primate had not long to live. For some time he was unable to travel on horseback and must be carried to and fro in a litter. The brain was less ready to do the bidding of the still eager will; his work was becoming a burden. With indomitable courage he had addressed himself to the task of attempting to reconcile the foreknowledge, predestination, and grace of God with the freewill of man. It was ever the man's habit to attempt great things. But he complained that, while once his stylus had found it difficult to keep pace with his ideas, he had now an unwonted difficulty in composition. As the strength ebbed away, he said wonderingly that he suffered no pain but only laboured under a total loss of appetite. With habitual self-control he who had once put constraint on himself to fast now controlled his body to eat. But it was the quiet and slow decay of all the vital functions. One care his fond monks could not persuade him to exercise over himself. He refused to surrender his lifelong habits of devotion, and to the end the life-worn man was carried into the oratory to take what part he was still able in Mass.

At last his monks could not deceive themselves any longer. On Palm Sunday one of them spoke out the

fear of all. " Father, we have come to understand
that you are about to leave the world and hold your
Easter feast at the court of your Lord." The old
man answered them : " I were glad, were such the
will of the Lord. Yet should I prefer if He were to see
fit that I might be suffered to continue here till such
time at least as I have solved a certain question about
the origin of the soul, because I know not whether
after my departure anyone will complete it." " The
search for truth still fires these great and restless
spirits even at the moment when they go into the
presence of the Truth. They prefer the love to the
possession, and on the threshold of heaven regret the
labour and the hope of earth." Nor do they ever
forget the necessity of the brethren, because to abide
may be more profitable for them.

On the late evening of the following Tuesday the
monks were chanting matins. In the archbishop's
chamber one of those who watched by the sick man
read the story of the Passion that by means of the
lesson for the day he might share in the common
service. When he had read " Ye are they which
have continued with Me in My temptations, and I
appoint unto you a kingdom as My Father hath
appointed unto Me, that ye may eat and drink at My
table," the labouring breath of the invalid warned
them that the end was near. They lifted him from
the bed and laid him, as the rule of his order commanded, on the sackcloth and ashes along the floor.
He died when the morning was beginning to break
on the 21st of April 1109.

He died as he had lived, with his thoughts busy
about the questions of man's soul and its relation to
16

God, with the habits of a lifetime of devotion as his
support to the end.

In the Introduction the attempt was made to point
out how the revived religious life within the Church
brought with it an inevitable collision with the State.
So soon as England had settled down after the Conquest, it was certain that, if the archbishop shared
this revived religious life, he would find himself in
conflict with the Norman king. It may be worth
while to attempt some estimate of what Anselm had
won by his compromise.

He had won for the Church a means of self-expres-
sion through which the revived life could make itself
felt in connection with the appointment of the
Church's leaders. The opportunity was given and
would now be valuable or useless according as the
spirit which guided the Church's action was pure or
otherwise. It may appear that, so long as the question
of election was not determined, nothing was finally
determined. Now the question of election was never
raised throughout the whole contest. It may be said
that, while Henry or any later king retained the power
to present his larderer or his chancellor to a bishopric,
he could be content to allow the Church to retain the
power of conferring by staff and ring the spiritual
authority on this candidate of his choice. He retained
the substance, and could therefore suffer the Church to
employ what forms it would. Yet it is one thing to
present a candidate where his election must be ratified,
and another to present him where the body which
confers upon him final authority has the power to
refuse that authority. Through the symbolic rite of
staff and ring the Church had the power to refuse the

king's candidate and to bring matters to a deadlock.
Should the king present to a bishopric a man whose
character or qualifications were a scandal to the office,
the Church had now the power to leave him un-
equipped for the functions to which he had been
chosen. It could protest not merely by low murmurs
but by a public act. That power and the knowledge
of its existence were able even to exert an indirect
influence on the election, for the king knew that he
must present the candidate of his choice to the public
verdict of the English Church. When therefore the
spirit which governed the Church was pure and high,
it was sure to exert its influence potently though
perhaps indirectly. When it was low, when bishops
recked little of their office, the king would be able to
ignore their verdict and do what he pleased. Anselm
had created the channel through which the spirit
which governed the councils of the Church had now
the opportunity to show itself. If the opportunity
were unused or misused, it was the fault of Churchmen
themselves, the sign of their degradation, the means of
their weakness.

In order to attain what he desired Anselm appealed
to Rome, and, since the victory was won by the aid of
Rome, helped to fasten on England a yoke which neither
we nor our fathers were able to bear. Because the action
of such men has been unscrupulously used in favour
of a theory of the papacy they neither knew nor held,
those who dissent from that theory often think it necessary to belittle the acts and question the motives of the
men whose action helped that authority. It were
fairer to realise the situation in which the man found
himself and the authority he did allow to Rome. He

found himself alone, unsupported not only by the barons of England but by his own suffragan bishops in an aim which he believed to be vital for the work of the Church of God in England. None in England realised its significance. Because he found no help there, he turned to Rome. He wanted liberty for Christ's Church, and Rome could aid him to win it. When Rome rendered such aid, it brought England into closer subjection to the central authority. Anselm aided that. He helped to give the Church of Rome its opportunity. He made it possible for the grandest experiment which was ever tried on earth, the experiment of a supreme tribunal which existed for the ends of Christ, to be tried in England. That the experiment failed was partly due to its impossibility and partly due to the fact that Rome could not rise to the greatness of the opportunity. It turned the opportunity which Anselm had helped to give it to base ends, and England cast it out with contumely.

It is also necessary to remember that the Rome of this century was not the Rome of later ages, not merely in the men who were its popes, but in the theory which good Churchmen held about its authority. They held and enforced very definite views about the limits of that authority. The Roman Curia was a centre where the best thought on questions which concerned the whole Church could be matured. When there was any general question to be considered, it was of manifest advantage that the Church should unitedly consider its whole bearing and issues, and that when action required to be taken the action should be simultaneous and unanimous. But the central authority did not engross all power so as to cramp the action of the Church in its national divisions. The communions in each land were free to determine their own local affairs with the clearer judgment which arose from their better knowledge. Anselm had no hesitation about promptly refusing to admit a papal legate within England. Perhaps his one experience with a legate had been too unfortunate to encourage its repetition. He insisted that no legate should enter England so long as the Archbishop of Canterbury was in the realm. The primate was as little inclined to surrender the liberty of the episcopate of England into the hands of a Roman bishop as into the power of a Norman king.

Nor did the Churchmen of that day dream that their loyalty to the head of their Church robbed them of the power to criticise its decisions. They paid Rome's verdict the compliment of thinking that it deserved discussion. Their liberty was no mere theory but was translated into practice. The freedom of language which loyal Churchmen of the time exercised is startling to anyone who chooses to study the writings of a mediæval saint at first hand and in something other than selections. Men like St. Bernard were not afraid, if they judged the pope mistaken or worse, to say it, and to say it publicly and roundly so that all men might hear.[1] And none counted them the worse Churchmen because they did these things. That dread of free discussion which is more often the symptom of weakness than of strength was unknown to the Middle Age men.

[1] It were a pleasure to hear, *e.g.*, the judgment of St. Bernard on a pope who blessed the labours of an editor of *La Croix*. It would be pungent.

The man however was even greater than his work. He enriched the religion of England, not merely by the specific victory he won, but by the character of the man who won it. The specific work of the Church and the ends for which it ought to work in England he brought forward more clearly; and, when those clashed in appointed strife with the condition of things as they were within the kingdom, his attitude was such as became a true Churchman. His unswerving rectitude, his transparent honesty in pursuit of the ends he desired, the furtherance of his purpose not by court intrigues but by simple appeal to reason and conscience, the nobility of his bearing toward those who opposed him, the charity of his judgment toward such as persecuted it, the simplicity with which he bore those persecutions, all these, because they were so full of the spirit of Christ, helped to make his aims more clear and more attractive.

Not less did he teach the Church a needed lesson as to her true weapons. In an age which believed in material force he flung himself with a superb confidence on the might of a meek and quiet spirit. His sweet reasonableness was his own chosen weapon and proved itself the most efficacious one. In a century which had begun to deal in excommunications with reckless-ness and to debase Church discipline into a means of seeking other than purely spiritual ends he did not have resort to that means of attack. When once he threatened to use it, the threat was sufficient. It was sufficient because he had never abused the weapon. Henry had measured the influence which the con-demnation of such a man could exert, and he could not afford wantonly to throw away that moral support to his throne. At the last moment, when he saw that nothing would move his archbishop, he yielded. Not only did Anselm, so far as he understood them, seek the things of Christ. He used, in order that he might attain them, the methods of Christ. One result is that it is impossible to sum up his contribution to England's religion by the statement that he won for it this thing or that. His contribution was himself, and to measure it rightly it is necessary to know him as well as his work.

But England owes Anselm one other benefit. She owes to his action that the worst brunt of the suffering, which every assertion of a great principle will always involve, fell not on her but on him. When one remembers the hideous war through which Germany needed to pass before the question between Church and State could be determined by a similar compromise, when one recalls such memories as Canossa, the Saxon rebellion which one pope fomented, and the treachery of Henry v. against his father which another pope did not venture to condemn, one recognises that it is in part to Anselm that England owes the absence of a similar struggle. The circumstances of course were different. The temptation was never so near Anselm as it was near Gregory and Urban to foment strife, to level excommunications, to release men from oaths of obedience when their release would help the Church's efforts. There might have been but few in England who would have supported him if he had taken that course; but it is to his honour and to England's profit that he never showed the least inclination to take such a course. He interposed on behalf of the coarse Rufus, after Rufus had worried him out of his kingdom. He interposed again to support Beauclerk, when his opposition might have made civil war more envenomed. England suffered only indirectly from its primate's loyalty to what he conceived to be his duty. It was himself who suffered most. Dragged from the studies which he loved, flung into a course of ecclesiastical negotiation and political bartering which were alien to his gentle spirit, torn away from the monastic life which was his delight into the turmoil of affairs, misunderstood, exiled, he never flung strife into the alien land, but bowed his head and submitted to suffer for the principles in which he believed. It had been well for the cause of the Church in England had his successors made themselves inheritors not merely of his principles but of his spirit.

# INDEX

# THE WORLD'S EPOCH-MAKERS.

*A Series of Biographical Studies dealing with Prominent Epochs in Theology, Philosophy, and the History of Intellectual Development.*

### EDITED BY OLIPHANT SMEATON.

Each Volume contains on an average 250 pages, and is published at $1.25. The Volumes will *not* appear in strict chronological sequence.

[*Continued on next page.*

# THE WORLD'S EPOCH-MAKERS—*continued.*

XIII. THE TWO BACONS AND EXPERIMENTAL SCIENCE. Showing how ROGER BACON prepared the way for FRANCIS BACON, LORD VERULAM. By Rev. W. J. COUPER, M.A.

XIV. SAVONAROLA. By Rev. G. M'HARDY, D.D.     [*Now ready.*

XV. LUTHER AND THE GERMAN REFORMATION. By Rev. Professor T. M. LINDSAY, D.D., U.F.C. College, Glasgow.
[*Now ready.*

XVI. CRANMER AND THE ENGLISH REFORMATION. By A. D. INNES, M.A.(Oxon.), London.     [*Now ready.*

XVII. CALVIN AND THE REFORMED THEOLOGY. By Rev. Principal SALMOND, D.D., U.F.C. College, Aberdeen.

XVIII. PASCAL AND THE PORT ROYALISTS. By Professor W. CLARK, LL.D., D.C.L., Trinity College, Toronto.

XIX. DESCARTES, SPINOZA, AND THE NEW PHILOSOPHY. By Rev. Professor J. IVERACH, D.D., U.F.C. College, Aberdeen.

XX. WILLIAM HERSCHEL AND HIS WORK. By JAMES SIME, M.A., F.R.S.E.     [*Now ready.*

XXI. WESLEY AND METHODISM. By F. J. SNELL, M.A.(Oxon.).
[*Now ready.*

XXII. LESSING AND THE NEW HUMANISM. Including Baumgarten and the Science of Æsthetics. By Rev. A. P. DAVIDSON, M.A.

XXIII. HUME AND HIS INFLUENCE ON PHILOSOPHY AND THEOLOGY. By Professor J. ORR, D.D., Glasgow.

XXIV. ROUSSEAU AND NATURALISM IN LIFE AND THOUGHT. By Professor W. H. HUDSON, M.A., Leland Stanford Junior University, California.

XXV. KANT AND HIS PHILOSOPHICAL REVOLUTION. By Professor R. M. WENLEY, D.Sc., Ph.D., University of Michigan.

XXVI. SCHLEIERMACHER AND THE REJUVENESCENCE OF THEOLOGY. By Professor A. MARTIN, D.D., New College, Edinburgh.     [*Shortly.*

XXVII. HEGEL AND HEGELIANISM. By Professor R. MACKINTOSH, D.D., Lancashire Independent College, Manchester.

XXVIII. NEWMAN AND HIS INFLUENCE. By C. SAROLEA, Ph.D., Litt. Doc., University of Edinburgh.

# WORKS BY PROFESSOR A. B. BRUCE, D.D.

## THE EPISTLE TO THE HEBREWS:

The First Apology for Christianity. An Exegetical Study. By A. B. BRUCE, D.D., Professor of Apologetics and New Testament Exegesis, Free Church College, Glasgow. Just published, Second Edition, in post 8vo, price 7s. 6d.

This book, the fruit of thirty years' study, is a companion volume to Professor Bruce's 'The Kingdom of God,' and 'St. Paul's Conception of Christianity.'

## ST. PAUL'S CONCEPTION OF CHRISTIANITY.

Post 8vo, price 7s. 6d.

'There need be no hesitation in pronouncing it the best treatment of Paulinism we have. . . . A book of first-rate importance.'—*Expositor.*

## THE KINGDOM OF GOD;

Or, Christ's Teaching according to the Synoptical Gospels. In post 8vo, Sixth Edition, price 7s. 6d.

' To Dr. Bruce belongs the honour of giving to English-speaking Christians the first really scientific treatment of this transcendent theme . . . his book is the best monograph on the subject in existence.'—Rev. JAMES STALKER, D.D., in the *British Weekly.*

' The astonishing vigour and the unfailing insight which characterise the book mark a new era in biblical theology.'—Professor MARCUS DODS, D.D.

## APOLOGETICS;

Or, Christianity Defensively Stated. In post 8vo, Third Edition, price 10s. 6d. In 'THE INTERNATIONAL THEOLOGICAL LIBRARY.'

' Dr. Bruce has won for himself the foremost place among apologists. . . . There does not exist in our language so satisfactory or original a treatment of the historicity of the Gospels, the claims of Jesus, and the significance of His appearance; nor have we so just and informing a criticism of the theories of primitive Christianity. . . . The Church at large will inevitably recognise Dr. Bruce's "Apologetics" as a volume of great and permanent value.'—*Expositor.*

## THE TRAINING OF THE TWELVE:

Or, Exposition of Passages in the Gospels exhibiting the Twelve Disciples of Jesus under Discipline for the Apostleship. In demy 8vo, Fifth Edition, price 10s. 6d.

' That minister who has not read "The Training of the Twelve" betrays an indifference to modern thought which is unpardonable."—President HARPER in the *Biblical World.*

## THE HUMILIATION OF CHRIST,

In its Physical, Ethical, and Official Aspects. In demy 8vo, Fourth Edition, price 10s. 6d.

' These lectures are able and deep-reaching to a degree not often found in the religious literature of the day; withal they are fresh and suggestive. . . . The learning and the deep and sweet spirituality of this discussion will commend it to many faithful students of the truth as it is in Jesus.'—*Congregationalist.*